BEST NEWSPAPER WRITING 1982

 **MODERN MEDIA INSTITUTE**
556 Central Avenue
St. Petersburg, FL 33701
813/821-9494

Other books in this series

Best Newspaper Writing 1979
Best Newspaper Writing 1980
Best Newspaper Writing 1981

BEST NEWSPAPER WRITING 1982

Winners

The American Society of Newspaper Editors Competition

Edited by Roy Peter Clark

Library of Congress Cataloging in Publication Data

Best Newspaper Writing, 1979 -
　　St. Petersburg, Fla., Modern Media Institute
Annual
"Winners, the American Society of Newspaper
Editors' competition," Editor: 1979 -　, Roy Peter Clark
Key Title: Best Newspaper Writing, ISSN 0195-895X

1. Journalism — Competitions.　I. Clark, Roy Peter.　II. Modern Media Institute.　III. American Society of Newspaper Editors.

PN4726.B38　　　　081　　　　80-646604
ISBN 0-935742-05-0

Copyright © 1982 by Modern Media Institute
556 Central Avenue, St. Petersburg, Florida

All rights reserved.
No part of this publication may
be reproduced in any form or by
any means without permission
in writing from the publisher.

Printed in the United States of America

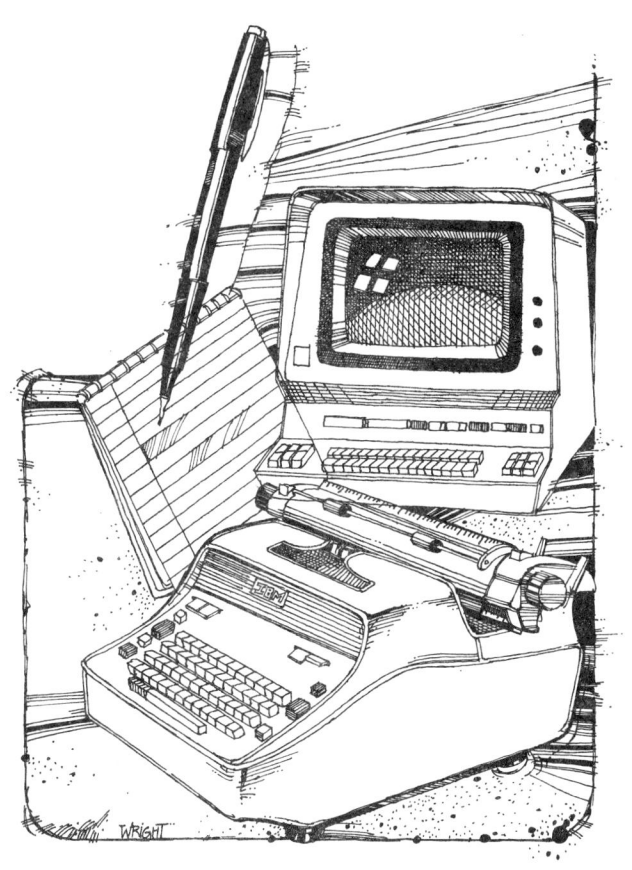

About this book

AUGUST, 1982

Each year since 1979, more writers, more teachers of writing and more readers who appreciate and enjoy good writing have bought *Best Newspaper Writing*. It goes as single copies and in shipments of as many as 200 to universities, to libraries, to newsrooms and to several thousand individuals in this country and around the world. Thus, *Best Newspaper Writing* is being read, and used, not only in the United States and Canada, but in Malaysia, South Africa, India, Thailand, Great Britain, Norway and Germany.

As in past years, *Best Newspaper Writing 1982* is a joint venture of the American Society of Newspaper Editors, the Modern Media Institute of St. Petersburg, Florida, and Dr. Roy Peter Clark, MMI's assistant director and editor of this series of books.

Five years ago, ASNE made better newspaper writing one of its key long-range goals. The following year it inaugurated a contest to pick the best writing in several categories from newspapers in the U.S. and Canada and to reward the writers with $1,000 prizes. Winning entries were assembled in *Best Newspaper Writing, Volume I*, along with Clark's notes and commentaries and interviews with the winning writers.

Each year the winners are chosen by a panel of editors that meets for several days to screen the nearly 700 entries in four categories — deadline and non-deadline writing, sports and commentary. Eighteen editors, under the chairmanship of David Laventhol, publisher of *Newsday* on Long Island, made up this 1982 contest panel:

H. Brandt Ayers, *Anniston* (Ala.) *Star*
Robert L. Bartley, *Wall Street Journal*
Judith W. Brown, *New Britain* (Conn.) *Herald*
Robert W. Chandler, *Bend* (Ore.) *Bulletin*
Michael Davies, *Kansas City Star and Times*
Katherine Fanning, *Anchorage Daily News*
Donald Forst, *Boston Herald American*
Murray J. Gart, *Washington Star*
Arthur Gelb, *New York Times*
Hal Gulliver, *Atlanta Constitution*
Alex S. Jones, *Greeneville* (Tenn.) *Sun*
James B. King, *Seattle Times*
David Lawrence Jr., *Detroit Free Press*
Richard H. Leonard, *Milwaukee Journal*
Maxwell McCrohon, Chicago Tribune Company
Robert C. Maynard, *Oakland Tribune*
James C. Squires, *Chicago Tribune*

 Dr. Clark, 34, was one of the first newspaper writing coaches and has been a national leader in the growing movement to make American newspapers more readable and more interesting. At MMI he conducts frequent writing seminars for newspaper professionals and for advanced liberal arts students seeking journalistic skills. But he also works with high school students, including many minority students, and conducts a pilot program in journalistic writing for fourth and fifth graders.

 Founded in 1975 by the late Nelson Poynter, chairman of the *St. Petersburg Times* and its subsidiary, *Congressional Quarterly*, the Modern Media Institute was bequeathed stock in The Times Publishing Co. in 1978. It invests its dividends in projects such as this book, Dr. Clark's writing seminars and programs in management, graphics and ethics for newspaper professionals and for students.

       Donald K. Baldwin, Director
       Modern Media Institute

Acknowledgments

The Wall Street Journal and William Blundell
Newsday and Patrick Sloyan
The Baltimore Sun and Theo Lippman Jr.
The Miami News and Tom Archdeacon
St. Paul Pioneer Press and H. G. Bissinger

Portraits by Jack Barrett
Illustrations by Michael Wright
Book design by Billie M. Keirstead

The cover for Best Newspaper Writing 1982 was created by Howard Sochurek, a New York photojournalist-engineer. Sochurek uses a computer-synthesizer to translate the gray values of photographs into vivid color combinations. When the desired colors have been assigned to each gray value, they are projected on a cathode ray tube and photographed with a Leicaflex camera on Kodachrome 64 film.

Contents

Introduction	**xi**
William Blundell Non-Deadline Writing	**1**
Patrick Sloyan Deadline Writing	**47**
Theo Lippman Jr. Commentary	**85**
Tom Archdeacon Sports Writing	**115**
H. G. Bissinger Finalist	**159**

Introduction

MAY, 1982

To improve the quality of the writing at newspapers, suggests one editor, we should fire all the bad writers and editors and hire good ones.

When I hear that, I am reminded of poet Sylvia Plath, a suicide victim, who during one period of sustained depression asked her psychoanalyst for a lobotomy.

"You're not going to get off that easy," he said.

None of us will get off easy in the struggle to rid newspapers of bad writing. This is a war of attrition, not a border skirmish.

That has become clear in the five years since Tim Hays, editor of the *Riverside Press-Enterprise*, uttered a single sentence at a meeting of top editors that was to spawn a national revival of interest in good writing.

It was October, 1976, and the directors of the American Society of Newspaper Editors were meeting in a conference room on a Honolulu beach. Tom Winship, editor of the *Boston Globe*, recalls that the editors "were in aimless discussion, anguishing over sagging circulation, poor lineage and general despondency about the future of newspapers."

Tim Hays interrupted the flagellants long enough to make an important contribution to American journalism. "Gents," he said, "why don't we, as editors, do what we are best equipped to do — improve the quality of the writing in our papers." Better writing, he argued, sells newspapers.

Much has happened in five years. Editors have recruited English professors, journalism teachers, novelists or veteran journalists as writing coaches in the newsroom. At least two newspapers, the *Boston Globe* and the *Tallahassee Democrat*, have created positions entitled Assistant Managing Editor for Writing.

Scores of newspapers, editors' associations and press clubs have organized writing seminars and workshops, some for the first time. Editors have created newsletters or bulletin boards to display examples of effective prose and to illustrate mistakes. Some papers have invested in "writers' libraries," small newsroom collections of excellent non-fiction and commentaries on writing.

Editors are finding better ways to collaborate with writers, making their way through the newsroom to congratulate a reporter for a good story or a copy editor for a good headline. Some papers are simply giving their best editors time to work with reporters.

In the absence of enlightened leadership, young reporters are discovering their own secret ways to get the advice and direction they crave. They show their copy to other reporters or to sympathetic editors in other departments. They pay their own way to regional meetings and seminars. They take classes at nearby universities to compensate for years of bad instruction or neglect.

An editor for a small Florida paper discussed the effects of a recent day-long writing seminar, sponspored by the Florida Press Association, on his staff. "A fresh commotion stirs out there among them," he said. "They're talking about writing techniques. They're conscious of things like form, tense and voice. They are in the process of improving themselves."

It would be misleading to paint too rosy a picture. The parsimony of publishers, the limitations of time and space, the crunch to get the paper out every day, the occupational negativism of editors, the conditioned cynicism of reporters — these remain as permanent obstacles to making the paper more responsible and readable.

But even these can be overcome by imaginative ideas. We need more of them. Last October I offered a list of ideas to a convocation of managing editors in Toronto. The list was designed to get them to think about the forces, human and institutional, that affect the quality of work in a newsroom. Some of these ideas were serious, others were wacky. (I've been told that the wacky ones are more useful than the serious ones.) Some were symbolic, meant to suggest something about the writing process or the relationship of writer and editor. Some would work well at one newspaper and be disastrous at another.

Here is an abbreviated version of the list:

1. Never refer to a writer as a "fixed cost."
2. Don't force a writer to become an editor in order to make good money.
3. Burn your red pencils. Mark pages in blue or black.
4. Encourage all editorial workers to write something during the year. Editors should try to write regularly.
5. Increase your editing staff at deadline by developing "swingers" who can edit when they are not working on their own stories.
6. Ask reporters to write one piece each month that serves as a change of pace from their beats. It may be funny, serious or experimental. Designate a regular place in the paper to display these.
7. Have writers suggest titles for their stories. Desk editors are still responsible for headlines. But writing a title can help a writer understand the focus of the story.
8. Create a "society of friends" within the newspaper, an atmosphere where writers and editors — even from different departments — can share ideas and react to each other's work.
9. Headline writers should study and practice haiku.
10. Writers should be encouraged to praise the work of desk editors. They need love too.

Someone should throw a party to introduce copy editors to reporters.

11. Writers, especially on longer pieces, should mark paragraphs that could be cut in a crisis. This will prevent samurai editing from the bottom and preserve good endings.

12. Create an "idea machine." Use a bulletin board, a newsletter or an editor to circulate ideas. Have an occasional brainstorming session.

13. Ask each reporter and editor to write one book review a year.

14. Consider paid sabbaticals for your best writers and editors.

15. Offer free seminars in writing and editing for local high school students. Get reporters or editors to teach them. Teaching will help them see their craft in a new way.

16. Once a month, interview a writer or editor on how he accomplished a successful story. Publish a transcript for the staff.

17. If an editor has contributed to a story in an exceptional way, consider putting his name on it.

18. Each day praise a headline that does not involve an easy play on words.

19. When working with young, inexperienced writers, don't work only with the final copy. Examine early drafts and even notebooks. Weak writing may derive from weak reporting.

20. Make it a firing offense for anyone at your paper to quote Kahlil Gibran.

Let me add another to the list: 21. Buy this book. If you already own a copy, buy another and give it to a friend. For *Best Newspaper Writing*, and the national writing competition it reflects, is another outgrowth of Tim Hays's 1976 proposal and the consequent activities of ASNE.

Almost 10,000 copies of the book have been sold — at a financial loss — in the last three years. The first three editions have been used by different readers in different ways.

* Reporters and editors use the book in the newsroom, to study and discuss story examples, and occasionally to question the decisions of the ASNE judges.

* Teachers, especially in journalism programs, use the text to encourage student writers and to expose them to discussions of writing techniques.

* This year a special issue of *Style*, a literary journal, will devote itself to scholarly discussions of newspaper writing. *Best Newspaper Writing* and its stories helped inspire that volume.

Each year, it is my privilege to pay close critical attention to the work of four or five strong writers. I get to interview them — usually by telephone — about their habits, frustrations and triumphs. I gather from these writers nuggets of advice which I find of value in my own teaching and writing. It has made me wonder why newspapers fail to conduct their own "How did you do it" style interviews with writers and editors who have done outstanding work.

This year, William Blundell of the *Wall Street Journal* taught me how to collect information and build a story structure around questions of time: What is the history of this topic? What is going on now? What does the future hold?

Tom Archdeacon, sports writer for the *Miami News*, described for me the type of reporting necessary to carry out a successful profile of a young athlete: Visit his home town, sit with his daddy on the front porch, visit his mother's grave, talk to every relative and neighbor, interview people in groceries, saloons and the Chamber of Commerce.

Humorist Theo Lippman of the *Baltimore Sun* explained how he finds obscure anniversaries in Chases' Calendar and uses them to develop witty political satires.

Patrick Sloyan of *Newsday*, who covered

the Sadat assassination, revealed how he can milk eyewitnesses — including other journalists —of details and description for his stories.

H.G. Bissinger, a finalist this year from the *St. Paul Pioneer Press*, described the arduous process of absorbing difficult information about a technical subject — aviation — and translating it for the reader.

An important part of my work involves talking about writing, reporting and editing with journalists across the country. From these discussions I get a sense of their values and concerns and get to examine and articulate my own.

Last year, for example, I got a phone call from an editor in South Dakota. He was organizing a workshop for publishers and editors. "What I want to know is this," he said. "If someone asks me why we should bother to improve the writing at our paper, what should I tell him?"

Perhaps I should have simply referred him to Tim Hays. Instead, I interpreted his question in a larger sense: "What do the writing improvers stand for?"

In an era of Pulitzer hoaxes and recycled advice columns it needs to be said — though it should be obvious — that we do not stand for dishonest writing. Dishonest writing is bad writing, no matter how beautiful the style, for it perverts clear communication and violates the trust that bonds the writer and reader.

We do not stand for self-indulgent overwriting, deceptive leads, the enforcement of stereotypes or those techniques more properly in the domain of fiction: composite characters, improved quotations, rearranged facts, invented authorial presence or the omniscient looking into minds.

We should be vigilant in protecting the craft from both the big liars and the little ones, those who select facts to distort the truth on behalf of a personal preference or special interest.

Having said that, I hope we will never replace the journalist's healthy skepticism with the destructive cynicism that is the sad stepchild of recent newspaper scandals. Anyone who has read Saul Pett or Mike Berger or Red Smith knows that you can tell the truth and tell it well.

Many misunderstand the writing movement by defining it too narrowly. Good writing is not a veneer to coat the facts. It is not style without substance. It is not all soft leads, metaphors and imagery.

We stand for clarity, relevance, humanity, hard work and the right word in the right place. Good writers are concerned with the needs of the reader. They want to explain complex issues without resorting to jargon. They believe that strong reporting makes good writing possible.

And consider this. When a group of journalists gets together to talk about writing, an interesting thing happens. Inevitably, the conversation turns to other related questions of editorial concern: How do you encourage better reporting? How do you enhance good writing with attractive graphics? How can management recruit and keep talented people? What are the writer's ethical responsibilities?

Five years has proven that the writing movement is the single most important lobby for editorial excellence in American journalism. Thank you, Tim Hays.

Roy Peter Clark
St. Petersburg, Florida

BEST NEWSPAPER WRITING 1982

William Blundell
Non-Deadline Writing

WILLIAM E. BLUNDELL, 47, is a national correspondent for the *Wall Street Journal* who lives in La Canada, California, and travels throughout the West writing about people, businesses and resources. He has worked for the *Journal* for 21 years in Dallas, New York and Los Angeles as a reporter, page one rewrite editor and Los Angeles bureau chief. He edited one book, *The Innovators*, and co-authored another, *Swindled*. Both were published by Dow Jones Books. Born in New York, Blundell graduated from Syracuse University in 1956 and did graduate work in journalism at the University of Kansas.

The life of the cowboy: drudgery and danger

JUNE 10, 1981

RAFTER ELEVEN RANCH, Ariz. — The lariat whirls as the man on horseback separates a calf from the herd. Suddenly, the loop snakes around the calf's rear legs and tightens. Wrapping a turn of rope around the saddle horn, the rider drags the hapless animal to his crew.

The flanker whips the calf onto its back, and the medicine man inoculates the animal. Amid blood, dust and bawling, the calf is dehorned with a coring tool, branded in an acrid cloud of smoke from burning hair and flesh, earmarked with a penknife in the ranch's unique pattern (cowboys pay more attention to earmarks in identifying cattle than to brands) and castrated. It is all over in one minute.

Jim Miller, the man in the saddle, smiles broadly as the released calf scampers back to his mother. Mr. Miller is 64 years old. Born and raised nearby, he has been working cows in Yavapai County since he was five. He will keep on until he can't throw a leg over a horse anymore. "It's all I know and I like it," he says.

The marks of his trade are stamped into his body: broken legs, a broken ankle, dislocated shoulder and elbow, a thigh torn open by a broken saddle horn. The fingers of the right hand are grotesquely broken, and he can't flex them fully. It is the roper's trademark, the digits that have been caught in the rope and crushed against the saddle horn, but Mr. Miller still wins roping competitions with that hand.

Jim Miller is a cowboy. There are still many cowboys in the West. Some wear black hats with fancy feather bands; they tear around in oversize pickups with a six-pack of Coors on the seat. These are small-town cowboys. They don't know anything about cows, and the only horses they know are under the hood.

Others become cowboys at sunset, shucking briefcases and threepiece suits for designer jeans, lizard-skin boots and silver buckles as big as headlights. Then they go to Western nightclubs to see what everyone else is wearing. They are urban cowboys, and the only bulls they know are mechanical ones.

Finally, there is a little band of men like Jim Miller. Their boots are old and cracked. They still know as second nature the ways of horse and cow, the look of sunrise over empty land — and the hazards, sheer drudgery and rock-bottom pay that go with perhaps the most overromanticized of American jobs. There are very few of these men left. "Most of the real cowboys I know," says Mr. Miller, "have been dead for a while."

HYPE AND ILLUSION

A big man with a ready laugh, he is both amused and exasperated by all the cowboy hype. "It almost makes you ashamed to be one," he says. "You've got doctors and lawyers and storekeepers runnin' around in big hats and boots." None, he intimates, would want to step into a real cowboy's place today; their image of the life is an illusion.

The typical ranch hand in this traditional cattle county, he says, is in his late teens or early 20s — so green he often doesn't know how to shoe his own horse — and must do all sorts of menial chores. Nobody can now afford the "horseback men," aristocrats of the saddle who spurned all ranch work that they couldn't do from the top of a horse except branding. Most hands are local boys who commute to work from nearby towns, as does Mr. Miller himself. With few exceptions, the bunkhouses full of "bedroll cowboys," wanderers from ranch to ranch over the West, are no more.

Some things haven't changed, though.

Punching cows, says Mr. Miller, "is still the lowest-paid job for what you have to know and do." In the '30s in Yavapai County, cowboys made $45 a month plus bed and board. The standard wage now is around $500 a month without bed and board. There is Social Security and the usual state coverage for job-related injuries, but there are no pension plans, cost-of-living adjustments, medical and life-insurance packages, or anything else.

Mr. Miller is one of the elite. His salary from Fain Land & Cattle Co., the family concern that operates the ranch, is $1,150 a month, but that is because he is the cowboss. The cowboss is the master sergeant of the ranch; he leads by example, works along with his men, and is in charge of day-to-day cattle operations. At various times the cowboss, or any other top hand, has to be a geneticist, accountant, blacksmith, cook, botanist, carpenter, tinsmith, surgeon, psychologist, mechanic, nurse and a few other things beside rider and roper. "There just isn't any point in a young fellow learnin' to be a top hand when he can make so much more today doin' practically anything else," the cowboss says sadly.

Then why do some still follow the life?

* * *

It is early morning on Mr. Miller's domain, more than 50,000 acres of rolling semi-arid dun hills and mountain slopes. The cowboss and two full-time hands work this country by themselves. They are going today to 7,800-foot Mingus Mountain to collect strays missed in the recent spring roundup. Mr. Miller surveys the land critically. Here and there the grama grass is greening up, but good summer rains will be needed to get the range in condition.

There is absolutely nothing that the cowboss can do about it except pray. The land is just too big. In almost every other occupation, man seals himself off from nature in factory or office tower, struggles to bend a little patch of it to his

will, or tries to wrest away its riches by force. But the cowboy knows he is only a speck on the vast plain, his works insignificant, his power to really control the land almost nil; nature herself is the only manager of the Rafter Eleven or any other ranch. So the cowboy learns to bow humbly before the perils and setbacks she brings, and to truly appreciate her gifts.

A big buck antelope squirms under a fence and sprints over the plain, hoofs drumming powerfully. "Now that's one fine sight," murmurs a cowboy.

The party is not sauntering colorfully over the hills on horseback. It is bouncing over them in a pickup. The cow ponies are riding comfortably behind in a special trailer; they, too, commute to work now. Though he grew up in the days of chuck wagons, line camps, bunkhouses and the great unfenced ranges, Mr. Miller is a strong believer in modern methods. He uses an electric branding iron because it is faster, and he will even use a trailer to take small groups of cattle from place to place on the ranch rather than drive them on foot. One pound sweated off a steer costs the ranch about 67 cents.

But he and every other experienced cowman draw the line at replacing the horse. There is a strange chemistry between horse and cow, a gentling effect, that he declares irreplaceable. "Some dummies around here tried motorcycles once. Didn't work worth a damn," snorts the cowboss. No machine, he adds, can ever duplicate the instincts and balletic ability of a fine cutting horse dancing into a herd to separate steer from heifer.

At Mingus Mountain the horses go to work. There is no glamorous dashing about on the plain, only a laborious, slow plod up a mountain canyon that is rocky, steep-sided, clogged with brush. Jagged tree branches jab at the riders. It is grueling, hazardous work, but a nice piece of high country is a valuable asset to any ranch here. In winter it is actually warmer for the cattle because the cold air settles in the valley below, and the nutritious scrub oak and other bushes are available year-round and grow above snow.

In a high clearing fringed by oak, juniper and pine, 18-year-old Troy Tomerlin pauses awhile, chewing on a twig, to consider his future. He can operate a backhoe and could make almost twice as much doing that as the $500 a month he gets now. "But I don't know how I'd like diggin' septic tanks day after day," he says. "Here I can see animals, work with animals, move around a lot of country. In an office you can't see nothin' but a desk, and I don't like people lookin' over my shoulder. Jim tells us what to do, and how you do it is up to you. I like that."

Suddenly, dark clouds begin to boil up over the mountain. Last week the cowboys were pelted by hail the size of golf balls, but that is just part of the job. Lightning, however, is much feared by any mounted man caught on the open plain, and many cowboys have been killed by it. Last summer a bolt barely missed Troy and knocked him unconscious. Other cowboys have been killed or crippled when their horses fell on them and leaped back up to gallop in panic with the rider entangled in rope or stirrup. "I've had three real good friends dragged to death that way," Mr. Miller says softly.

LARIATS USED SPARINGLY

The clouds pass over harmlessly and 18 head coaxed out of the rocks and brush are driven toward the plain. Tommy Stuart, a fine rider with rodeo experience, crashes through brush again and again to divert straying animals. The men cry out to the cattle in a strangely musical series of yips, calls and growls. Tommy has to rope a balky calf, the only time anyone uses his lariat; the cowboy who does so frequently doesn't know how to drive cattle, Mr. Miller says.

The trick, he says, is to watch the way their ears are pointing and so anticipate their direction. Mr. Miller also rests cattle frequently on drives to let cows and calves "mother up" so they're more easily driven, or to calm trotty (nervous) animals. "If you don't rest them," he says, "they'll start to run, they'll get hot, then they'll get mad. Then there's no turning them. You've got to keep your cattle cool."

The fall weaning is a particularly sensitive time. Separated from their mothers until the maternal bond is broken, the calves, now sizable, are under stress that can cause pneumonia. When the animals finish days of bawling and finally lie down, the sound of a car, a dog's bark, even the cry of a night bird, may set them back on their feet and running in stampede, mowing down fences, crushing each other in the pileup of bodies. This happened to Mr. Miller twice when he was cowboss on the big Yolo ranch.

Nothing untoward happens on this drive, and the riders finally reach the plain. No chuck wagon rolls up with a bewhiskered Gabby Hayes type ready to ladle out son-of-a-bitch stew — classically, a concoction of cow brains, tongues, hearts, livers and marrow, with a handful of onions thrown in to conceal the taste. Instead everyone rumbles back to the ranch house and the cowboss himself fixes lunch for his men: steaks, beans, bread smothered in gravy, and mayonnaise jars full of iced tea.

HOW TO GET FIRED

By tradition, the cowboss looks out for his cowboys and hires and fires them himself. Besides incompetence, two things will get you fired by Jim Miller: abuse of horses and bellyaching. The latter is a breach of a cowboy code still in force. For $500 a month, the ranch expects and almost always gets total and uncomplaining loyalty to the outfit. Unionism is an utterly alien concept to cowboys; if a man doesn't like his boss, his job or anything else, he quits on the spot.

Firing is as simple. There are no hagglings over severance pay, no worries about employee lawsuits. "I just tell them, 'This is it,' and they go," says Mr. Miller.

Once, when a cowboss needed good hands, he would just drop in at the Palace Bar on Whisky Row in Prescott. This was the hiring hall and water hole, full of men who had been on the range for months and were "getting drunker'n seven hundred dollars," as Mr. Miller puts it. He doesn't go there anymore. "Now it's full of hippies and such as that, people who don't know a horse from a cow," he says. Instead, cowboys call him at home when they need work.

Lunch is over, and the men get off their rumpsprung old chairs and go out to nurse a young heifer internally damaged when calving. If they don't get her up to walk she will die.

* * *

At the offices of the Rafter Eleven, Bill Fain has been told by his computer that the cattle he soon will sell will have cost about 68 cents a pound to raise and fatten. He expects to get 67 cents for them. That's the cattle business today, says Mr. Fain, vice president of Fain Land & Cattle and the third generation of his family on this ranch. And such thin margins make men like Jim Miller particularly important.

The cowboss is considered one of the canniest judges of livestock in the area, and buys the registered bulls and replacement heifers for the ranch. It is he, more than anyone else, who maintains, the quality of the herd. He coaxes an 80 percent calf crop out of the 700 mother cows here, a good ratio. He does not overburden the land, letting it rest and renew.

"Our product isn't cattle. It's grass," says Mr. Fain, "and Jimmy knows that. A lot of people can rope and ride and love the life, but there are damned few left who can do all the things he does."

Outside, cars whiz by on the road that crosses what used to be called Lonesome Valley. Some 6,000 people live there now because the Fains, trying to diversify out of an increasingly risky reliance on cattle, sold a piece of the ranch to a developer who built a town on it. The Fains developed another piece themselves.

This has made the cowboy's job harder. Cattle have been shot and cut up on the spot with chain saws by shade-tree butchers who throw the pieces in the back of a pickup and drive off, leaving head and entrails. People tear down cattle feeders for firewood, shoot holes in water tanks, breach fences to maliciously run down calves. "People and cattle don't mix," concedes Mr. Fain. "It's a sick thing," says Jim Miller, and there is icy anger in his blue eyes.

Meanwhile, the old family ranches are being sold, most of them to investors who don't know one end of a Hereford from the other and are more interested in tax shelter than running a good spread. This has driven ranchland prices so high that a young man who really wants to raise beef either can't afford to buy or has no hope of getting a return on his investment. "I really can't see much future in the cattle business," Mr. Miller says.

COUGARS AND GRASSHOPPERS

Perhaps not. But around Yavapai County the cycle of ranch life continues unchanged on the surviving family spreads. In Peeples Valley, cougars have taken 15 calves this year and lion hunter George Goswick is tracking them through the Weaver Mountains. In the pastures, mares are heavy with foals; in time, some will find their way into the gentling hands of Twister Heller, the horse breaker. On the Hays ranch, owner John Hays is stabbing a wild-eyed Hereford bull in the rump with a needle full of antibiotics and fretting about the grasshoppers that are all over the property. There is too much ranch and too many hoppers, so he must simply accept them.

At evening, Jim Miller comes home to a house and five rural acres with horse corral outside Prescott. He and his wife, Joan, have lived here 10 years; for the first 27 years of their marriage they lived on the local ranches he worked, raising four sons and two daughters, teaching all to rope and ride. None has followed in his footsteps because there isn't any money in it.

Next year, when he's 65, Mr. Miller plans to quit as cowboss at the Rafter Eleven and start collecting Social Security. But he says he will never stop working. Few men around here who have spent their lives on a horse seem able to get off. Jim's friend Tom Rigden still rides roundup and castrates calves on his ranch, though he has been blind for almost eight years.

Mr. Miller doesn't expect any trouble finding day jobs on ranches. At a time when there are so few real cowboys left, he says, there is always work for a top hand.

Observations and questions

1) Verbs fall into three categories: active voice, passive voice, and forms of the verb *to be*. Good writers write in the active voice, but know how and when to use other verb forms as well. Consider Blundell's lead. In the first two paragraphs he relies on the active voice: the lariat whirls, the loop snakes and tightens, the rider drags, the flanker whips and the medicine man inoculates. Attention rests on the cowboy as agent. Then, in midstream, Blundell shifts the focus. He turns to the passive and shows the animal as receiver of action. The calf is dehorned, branded, earmarked and castrated. Then a final short sentence defines simple state of being: "It is all over in one minute." Analyze the rest of Blundell's work in terms of his use of verbs.

2) Consider your own work. Take a story you have written; underline each verb that you use. Mark the verb active, passive or *to be*. Do you depend too heavily on the verb *to be* or the passive? Do you know how to manipulate verb voice to create specific effects in your story?

3) Blundell uses lines of time to organize his stories. Examine this piece and mark those places where the writer deals with the present, the past and the future. Is this a satisfying structure for the story?

4) To give his prose a sense of immediacy, Blundell writes in the present tense. Rewrite passages of Blundell's prose in the past tense. Compare the two versions and decide which you like better.

5) Blundell uses quotations sparingly in this

story. Look closely at the words of cowboy Jim Miller. How do these quotations help us understand the life of the contemporary cowboy? How do they enhance our impression of Jim Miller's character?

6) A reader of this story has dozens of images in his mind of what cowboy life is like. These may come from film, television or fiction. Blundell calls being a cowboy "the most overromanticized of American jobs." Western clothes and music are popular, as is the hard fighting, hard drinking, hard loving mystique of the cowboy. Consider how Blundell deflates this image.

7) Write a story or series under the rubric *Life on the Job.* Take an occupation that has a certain mystique about it: pilot, lifeguard, investigative reporter, criminal lawyer, actor, musician. Spend a day or two on the job with such a person and write about the reality of the job versus its romanticized image.

The fatal fraternity of Northwest loggers

DECEMBER 8, 1981

KALAMA, Wash. — Let us say that you work in an office building with 1,000 people and that every day at least two are hurt on the job. Some suffer such ghastly wounds — multiple compound fractures, deep cuts severing muscle, sinew and nerve, shattered pelvises — that they may never return to their old posts. And every six months or so, a body is taken to the morgue.

Almost anywhere, this would be called carnage, and a hue and cry would be raised. But in the big-tree logging woods of the Pacific Northwest, it is simply endured with what logger-writer Stan Hager has called "proud fatalism," and few outside the loggers' trade even know of it. Miners trapped behind a cave-in draw national media attention, but in the dim rain forests men fall singly and suddenly. There aren't any TV cameras.

Increased stress on training and safety in recent years has helped. But death and injury rates still are extraordinarily high in part because loggers are an almost suicidally prideful and tradition-bound group, hooked on danger and suspicious of new equipment and techniques.

RESISTANCE TO CHANGE

"There's tremendous macho, and I can't imagine any group of men more resistant to change," says Joel Hembree, the safety coordinator for local 3-536 of the International Woodworkers of America, which represents loggers and millworkers in southwest Washington. The union, he adds, is thus in the awkward position of pushing measures that many of its own members oppose. "We're a bunch of dirty S.O.B.'s for trying to jam safety down their throats," he says.

In the forest, a few loggers sit in a bus reeking of old socks, wet wool and tobacco smoke, grousing about safety. "They've already got us decked out like Christmas trees," growls Howard "Spider" Mason, a 36-year-old Weyerhaeuser Co. "timber faller," or cutter, displaying a pair of heavy water-soaked leg protectors the law now says he must wear. Another logger recites a poem about the idiocies of the safety people that concludes, "Who's going to protect us against our protection?"

Even if the loggers did festoon themselves with every safety gadget available, the forest has a hundred treacherous ways to get them anyway. "To you the forest is a pretty place," says a union staffer. "To our guys it's dark, it's scary and it's out to hurt them."

Men are crushed to death by trees that simply fall over without being touched, or speared through by broken branches that fall 250 feet on a windless day, or maimed by rocks bouncing down hillsides.

The forest also is unforgiving of error, and a moment's carelessness can wound or kill. About 15,000 men are usually working in the Washington woods; over the past three years they have suffered a total of almost 28,000 injuries and 75 deaths. "It's you against the trees," says a veteran woodsman.

This toll is viewed with stoicism. Spider Mason, tall, dark and talkative ("Spider wore out two pair of lips before he was 18," says a coworker), keeps his buddies laughing at his banter. But he is serious about the hazards of the job. "You go to work every day knowing death is in the trees," he says. "Your family knows it; my wife doesn't want to hear anything about what I do. But a logger has to *enjoy* danger or he isn't a logger."

Generations of the Mason clan have gone into the forest and, as with so many other families, it has made them pay for their fascination with it. The forest has already killed Spider Mason's uncle, grandfather, father and brother. The forest has also taken a big price from the town of Hayesville, N.C., population about 300; Clarence Stamey, woods business agent for the IWA local here, comes from Hayesville and can think of 10 fellow townsmen who have come to the Northwest woods to die. He may have forgotten a name or two, he adds.

The trade-off for all this? Membership in a fraternity.

* * *

At 4 a.m. bedroom lights go on in Kalama, Longview and smaller lumber towns — "the three-house, two-bar places," one logger calls them — buried in the green spires of the Cascade Range. A little later, the sleepy men board their "crummies," the aptly named crew buses that take them to their camps. All wear a uniform that hasn't changed in decades: caulked boots, heavy trousers cut off near the tops of the boots, work shirt, suspenders (no logger wears a belt), and usually a full beard or a brushy mustache.

By dawn the chain saws are snarling in the woods. The loggers won't get back home until dark — or well after dark as the days grow shorter. In between, they do some of the hardest physical work in American industry. Toiling "in the pit," at the bottom of infernally steep slopes, "choker-setters" struggle to fit 100-pound collars around the logs to be dragged uphill on one-inch cables grinding overhead. Laden with 50 to 100 pounds of gear, the timber fallers crawl up and down hills clogged with man-high brush to find their trees. In summer there is heat exhaustion, in winter the sheer misery of constant rain or snow.

It is the ability, and the will to endure such work that bind Northwest loggers together. To them, the loggers of the Southeast, where the trees are smaller, the land flatter and the climate benign, are mere woodchoppers. *"This* is logging," brags one foreman, indicating a virgin forest where monster Douglas firs eight feet in diameter and 250 feet tall can still be found. Nine miles east, Mount St. Helens rises like a white wall, its shattered summit banked in mist.

This is a male society. Few women apply for work requiring such great upper-body strength, and those who do confront a relentlessly macho atmosphere. At one camp men chose lots to sit next to a woman choker setter on the crummy so they could harass her on the way home; she quit. A logging supervisor says, "The idea that a woman possibly could do what they do — well, it just kills them."

Few blacks work in the Northwest woods, either. Many loggers are from Southern families, and deeply ingrained racial attitudes persist. An old logger, arms covered with chainsaw scars, says earnestly, "A while back, they tried real hard to get some of those niggers up here to work, but they didn't stick. I don't know why."

Everyone who enters the woods is hazed crudely and unmercifully. Does he have big ears? He is Dumbo forever. Is he a newlywed? Slip some dirty pictures into his empty lunchbox so his bride will find them. Put rocks in his gear bag, give him grueling, unnecessary chores to do. Test him. "The tender young boys don't last," says Spider Mason. One called Dimples so displeased the veteran logger he worked with that the latter picked him up overhead and threw him uphill with instructions never to return. He didn't.

In work so dangerous, it is vital to cull the unfit and the incompatible. A streak of meanness in the hazing often is the first sign that a man is on the way out, says Jack Coady, the superintendent of Weyerhaeuser's District 6, comprising 142,000 acres of forest east of Kalama. The victim may have his lunch destroyed or his clothes set afire; then another man may invite him behind a tree for a faceful of knuckles. Finally the hook tender — the boss union logger — may simply say, "Go on down the road. We don't want to see you anymore."

If a man is a good worker but cannot get along with his fellows, Mr. Coady will bluntly tell him that he is fouling up and that if he can't adjust to his next crew, he will be run off. Bluntness is always the loggers' way. "It's good, clean communication, one on one," he says. "No dancing around, no politics. Logging is an open society and that's one reason I like the industry so much."

The woods are full of men who have repeatedly quit the miseries and dangers but who keep coming back. The open, rough camaraderie, the knowledge that they can do work others quail from out of fear or weakness, forges a sense of community they cannot find outside.

Greg Kruger, a strapping, fair-haired logger, says, "The beauty of the woods is that if you can do a damn good job, you can be any man you want, you can wear a clown suit or a tuxedo to work if you want. You'll get razzed to death — but you're accepted. You belong."

In 1974 a basketball-sized rock glancing off a canyon wall crushed Greg Kruger's left side. (One of the men who carried him out quit on the spot when he saw the wounds.) Now Greg's arm is a mass of scar tissue, and a piece of shattered pelvis still floats around inside him. Partly disabled, he works in the office at South Camp, the headquarters of District 6.

Work is somehow found for many men hurt seriously on the job — even though this may involve violating contract rules that require filling slots by seniority. Union representatives and company supervisors just look the other way; it is more important that the fraternity to which both belong takes care of its own. As for Greg Kruger, he wishes he could set choker again. But it is enough just to be here, still a member in good standing.

* * *

Thirty of the 210 men at South Camp are in a little contest. Divided into three groups of 10, they have been promised that if any group goes six months without an injury, the men and their wives will get a free dinner. "Shoot, they'll never collect," mumbles the logger. Three men on two of the teams were hurt within days after the list had gone up, thus having to start the six-month cycle all over again.

The 30 are South Camp's crack crew of timber fallers, the loggers who have the greatest risk of death. This camp hasn't lost a cutter in many years, but every old-timer on the crew knows someone who has been killed at this exacting craft. Conversation with fallers is a litany of tales about crushed skulls, broken backs, legs half-severed by chain saws. They also suffer scarred eyeballs from wood particles flying out of saw cuts, permanent hearing loss from saw noise far in excess of maximum federal standards, and damage to the capillaries and nerves of the hand because of vibration, damp and cold.

SAFETY RECORD

This is called white hand, and Roy Palmer has it badly. At times his hand turns a corpse-like white, and he loses feeling in it, a dangerous thing that Roy and the others shrug off. "You just clamp your fingers on with the other hand, and once in a while you burn it on the muffler (of the chain saw) till your glove starts to smoke," he says cheerfully.

At 62 and near retirement, Roy is still one of the most productive cutters. He went 27 years without an injury, an incredible record. Men have died around him, and once a partner, immobilized in front of an oncoming log when his foot got stuck, screamed to Roy to cut his leg off (he cut him out of his boot instead). But Roy himself escaped until recently.

He tore his hand on a running saw last year. And this past July, he had another accident while he was cutting a fallen tree into log lengths. When a tree is lying on uneven ground, it is full of areas of tension and compression called binds. After these are cut through, the sections can writhe like snakes or swing uphill or down, pivoting on rocks or stumps and crushing anything in their way. Roy Palmer fell as a tree moved, and his saw cut through muscles near his ankle and halfway into the bone.

There are scores of ways that loggers can die from a single mistake, and they are acutely conscious of the need for total concentration. Gary Trople, who is going through a divorce, says his production drops when marital troubles are on his mind because he won't touch a tree without having his entire attention on it.

Like others, he has a love-hate relationship with his job. Even at six, he wanted to be a timber faller; "I'd take a hatchet and beat on some of those little-bitty pine poles till they fell down," he recalls. But four months after he started in the woods, a snapping cable threw him against a stump, crushing his ribs, fracturing his skull and breaking his back in three places. "I swore I'd never come back," he says. "Five months later I was back. I went in the Army for four years and swore I'd never come back. Here I am."

VALUE OF NARROW ESCAPES

Not long ago he felled a tree that brushed another tree in its descent, bending it like a 220-foot catapult. The tree sprang back to fire a deadly hail of broken limbs at him, but he escaped with lacerations. "Most of the time that would kill you," says his supervisor, a ginger-bearded logger named Jack Davis. But he adds that without close calls a faller can be lured into a false sense of security that may prove fatal. Jerry Baldwin, a young cutter, listens dubiously. "When I have a close call," he says, "I just go home and shake for a while."

For this extra ration of danger, fallers get some of the top pay in the woods — $30,000 in a good year for an hourly paid union man, more for a good "gyppo busheler," a cutter working for a nonunion contractor and paid by the amount of wood he can lay on the ground.

Their psychic income is the satisfaction that comes from conquest of the great forest giants, and fallers always remember their biggest trees. "Lay one of those big dudes down just where you want, save it all, and you've done something damn few men anywhere can do," says one. A bad job that splits or breaks a tree can destroy 90 percent of its lumber value.

"UPHILL! UPHILL!"

In a virgin grove, Elmer Osborne and Paul Cline are working on a tree that was growing before Columbus sailed. It is about seven feet thick and 240 feet tall. After making the undercut, a thick wedge of wood removed in the desired direction of fall, Elmer cuts through the other side until only a thin slab of "holding wood" supports hundreds of tons above. Its equilibrium altered, the tree creaks, the wood tears away, and Elmer yells, "Uphill!" (No one yells, "Timber!" anymore.) The fir falls slowly, striking with a mighty *whump* that shakes the earth. It is a perfect fall, saving intact about $6,000 in logs and much more in lumber value at retail. "I'll take that one. That's a good one," Elmer says with a broad smile. It doesn't matter now that an hour earlier a 160-foot dead tree falling the wrong way almost wiped him out.

Such scenes grow rarer. On the private lands of the big timber companies, the enormous trees of the virgin forest are quickly disappearing; in their place are strange, monotonous woods that seem almost dead by comparison — filled with trees of the same height, thickness and species, all planted by men. They will never be allowed to reach the size of the old giants because that is uneconomical. Harvesting them will be far safer than working in the virgin forest, with its treacherous rotting trees, snarls of interlocking top branches, and leaning trees. But much of the glamour of logging will fade with that natural forest, too.

"That's why I've got pictures of the biggest trees I've cut," says Jack Davis, the supervisor. "For the kids, so they can see what it was really like. The day is coming when men in these woods will laugh if you tell them there were really trees 10 feet thick here.

Observations and questions

1) Stories may contain paragraphs of high interest and of low interest. For example, the writer may present a paragraph of statistics to the reader. Perhaps this paragraph provides important evidence, but it may not hold the reader's attention as would a colorful anecdote, a crisp description or a telling quotation. The good writer rewards the reader by following paragraphs of low interest with ones of high interest, thus keeping the attention of the reader and building the momentum of the story. Search for examples of this technique in Blundell's work. Experiment with it yourself.

2) Halfway through this story, Blundell concludes that the loggers form a kind of fraternity. We may be struck by the obvious differences between a college fraternity and the society of loggers. Yet the writer sees clear similarities and shows them to the reader. Using evidence presented by Blundell, discuss the implications of comparing the society of loggers to a fraternity.

3) Most readers of the *Wall Street Journal* lead lives different from that of the Northwest logger. Many work in office buildings. Consider how Blundell lures his readers into the story by putting them in a familiar setting and by addressing them directly: "Let us say that you work in an office building. . . ."

4) The lead ends with the word *morgue*. How does that word set the tone for the story? Consider those incidents and anecdotes that illustrate the dark violence of the forest and the "proud fatalism" of the loggers.

5) Study the quotations attributed to Spider Mason. Discuss the differences between these and the ones attributed to cowboy Jim Miller in the previous story.

6) Blundell's paragraphs seem longer than the norm for newspaper stories. Examine the structure of Blundell's paragraphs. Do they pass the test of unity, coherence and development?

7) The points of emphasis in a paragraph are at the beginning and end. Discuss Blundell's paragraphs in these terms. Does he use the beginnings and ends of paragraphs to emphasize dramatic or important points? Consider your own work. Does appealing information get lost in the middle of paragraphs? Rewrite them.

8) The same technique applies to sentences. Discuss how Blundell gives weight to certain words by their placement in the following sentences:

> Not long ago he felled a tree that brushed another tree in its descent, bending it like a 220-foot catapult.

> In 1974 a basketball-sized rock glancing off a canyon wall crushed Greg Kruger's left side.

> In a virgin grove, Elmer Osborne and Paul Cline are working on a tree that was growing before Columbus sailed.

Indians save land from white man's dam

DECEMBER 17, 1981

FORT MCDOWELL, Ariz. — The 360 Yavapai Indians on this small reservation, the shrunken remnant of thousands who once lived on 10 million Arizona acres, have won their first great victory over the white man. He wanted to stuff some $33 million into their pockets. They told him to get lost.

The money would have been paid for a patch of Yavapai desert flooded by the proposed Orme Dam, the keystone of a $1 billion federal water project that practically every element of Arizona's political and economic power structure has lusted after for 13 years. But the huge dam at the confluence of the Salt and Verde rivers would have inundated up to 17,000 of the 25,000 acres the tribe has left, and forced its relocation.

So the Yavapai (pronounced yah-vuh-PIE), who were never even consulted about the dam when it was first authorized in 1968, dug in for a last stand. They lobbied in Congress, marched on a "trail of tears" to the state capitol, and picketed Sen. Barry Goldwater at a public appearance. "This was our last piece of homeland," says tribal chairman Norman Austin. "There was no other place for a people who had been sent wandering over the desert for so many years."

GOVERNMENT CAVES IN

The government, of course, could have just condemned the property, kicked out the Yavapai, and paid them off anyway. But confronted by their refusal to sell voluntarily at any price, by rising public sympathy for them, and by the certainty of a lawsuit by the Indians and their environmentalist allies (the dam would have drowned the south Verde's riparian habitat, bald-eagle nesting sites and archaeological ruins), the dam's proponents are caving in.

Now most of them have reversed course, to support an alternative plan that won't affect the Yavapai. The final decision will be made by Interior Secretary James Watt, who has already informally backed the alternative; official approval won't be announced until environmental-impact statements are completed, but it is generally agreed that the Orme Dam is dead.

"It's pretty amazing," says Lawrence Aschenbrenner, an attorney for the Native American Rights Fund who aided the Yavapai in their struggle. "All sorts of well-intentioned people told the Yavapai they were sticking their heads in the sand, that if they'd just negotiate, they could make a heck of a deal. The $33 million was a tentative bargaining offer, really. What these pople have done is an example to other tribes who can now say, 'By God, if we get together and don't give up, we can win too.' "

Meanwhile, on their mountain-ringed piece of Sonoran desert, the Indians celebrate because they don't have to take Uncle Sam's money. When news of Secretary Watt's preliminary opinion was announced a month ago some elders wept or cried out with joy. "I ran down here hollerin' and my daughter said, 'Are you sick? Are you crazy?' " recalls Bessie Mike, a 73-year-old basket weaver.

A great billowing woman in a print dress, she sits under a tree outside a tiny cinderblock home painted lilac; a rusting Plymouth Fury is sinking into the desert nearby. She has just received $1,100 for basketry it took her four months to make. Couldn't she use $100,000 or so? Why not sell the land? "This is our place," she says simply.

Not all Yavapai opposed the dam. One living off the reservation, Michele Guerrero of Mesa, has publicly criticized the tribe's decision, saying that the money could have been of immeasurable help in raising the tribe's standard of living and educational level. Many whites also find the decision incomprehensible for the same reason. "I still think they made a mistake," says one state official. "Just think of what they could have done for themselves with all that money."

But some Yavapai cheerfully admit they would probably just blow much of it on a spending binge. One tells of a cousin who got $1,500, part of an overall $5.1 million land-claim settlement distributed among the tribe in the mid-1970s. He splurged on an expensive Western outfit, including red boots, started nipping on a jug, and extended grants and loans to hangers-on. He awoke the next morning sans money and everything else. Even the boots were gone.

So to the Yavapai, the white man's money is ice, but the land is diamonds. A profound and mystical connection to that land, something many whites don't comprehend, is at the root of the Yavapai resistance. In a tribal vote five years ago, 144 of them voted to hold the land and 57 voted to sell it, with most of the latter votes apparently coming from tribal members living off the reservation. Today, it is difficult to locate anyone living at Fort McDowell who admits he voted to sell.

Like other tribes, the Yavapai hold their land in common, not as individual plots, and they view it as an integral part of their religion and culture. "Land should not belong to people — people belong to the land," says Virginia Mott, an outspoken opponent of the dam.

Tribal religion and culture have been in decline, slowly eroded by neglect and by white influences. The Yavapai tongue is dying out, the last medicine man is gone, and knowledge of the old faith and customs resides mostly among the elders. But enough of the Yavapai way remains in the tribal consciousness to make even the thought of drowning the land a desecration.

HONORED DEAD

There are prayer grounds here consecrated by medicine men of old. There is the neatly tended cemetery, all graves aligned to face the sacred mountain called Four Peaks. To the Yavapai, the dead remain a part of the community, and to disturb them would be deeply troubling. (One grave holds the honored bones of Carlos Montezuma, a Yavapai physician and a powerful spokesman for all Indian interests until his death in 1923. He had predicted that the whites one day would try to build a dam that would flood the reservation. "White people's heads are long," he wrote. "They can see many years ahead" about the future need for a dam.)

Finally, there are the Kakakas, the secretive Old Ones who are the guardians and protectors of the Yavapai. In tribal lore, they are tiny people, three or four feet tall, immortal, and live on Four Peaks, Superstition Mountain, and Red Mountain, as well as in ruins at Fort McDowell that the Yavapai avoid. Flood out the Kakakas? Unthinkable.

Beyond their reverence for the land itself, the Yavapai also harbor a historically justified skepticism about white promises. In the 1860s the U.S. cavalry promised them food, clothing and land if they would settle near Army forts; they got starvation and smallpox instead. Lumped in with the far more warlike Apache (they still are called Mohave-Apache, though their language is entirely different), they were mowed down by Army rifles at Skeleton Cave, Bloody Basin, Skull Valley.

LANDING ON RESERVATION

Rounded up again on land they were told would be theirs, they were again displaced and sent on a forced march of 180 miles to the Apache reservation at San Carlos. Many died. They finally got their own reservation here in

1903 and have clung to it since, despite repeated threats to move them into the nearby Salt River reservation with their ancestral foes, the Pimas.

Thus, they were wary of white promises about the benefits they would enjoy from the dam. One was exclusive concessions for boating and fishing on the lake it would form. Beyond the fact that Yavapai hate fish and don't like still water, it wasn't made clear until recently that the lake level would fluctuate so drastically that the place would be a mud flat much of the time, which would have left the Indians operating the only landlocked marina in the U.S.

Though they apparently have won the fight against the Orme Dam, the Yavapai and their allies have little confidence that they will be left alone from now on. Carolina Butler, a feisty white housewife from Scottsdale who has aided the Yavapai from the beginning, wants an endangered-Indian law to protect small tribes everywhere from destruction by such projects. Tribal member Phil Dorchester, noting that water wells in Phoenix and Scottsdale have been poisoned by chemicals, says fatalistically, "They'll come up here sooner or later to try to get more water from the Verde. They'll have to."

The young will have to be vigilant, says John Williams, 77 and wheelchair-bound. "I am a man of rubber now," he says, indicating his useless legs, "but I would tell the young people this: The God behind blue heaven made this land for his people. Hold it. Put writing on papers. Do not sell it. Do not lease it. Pass it down. All this my own father told me too."

Observations and questions

1) Discuss Blundell's topics and their appropriateness for the *Wall Street Journal*. Aren't there strong cultural divisions between the values of those who read the *Journal* and the subjects of Blundell's stories? Discuss the similarities between the cowboys, the loggers and the Indians? Aren't they all "shrunken remnants" of past societies? They preserve old ways and values — both positive and negative. They seem suspicious of "progress" and technology.

2) The *Wall Street Journal* is admired as one of the best written papers in the country. The stories on page one are praised and widely read. Many are rewritten, to some extent, by a bank of talented editors. Some critics of the *Journal* complain that these page one stories follow something of a formula and seem "homogenized" at times. Read *WSJ* carefully for a month, paying special attention to the page one stories. Is there a formula? Do you think the criticism is justified?

3) Contrast the writing on page one of the *Journal* to page one of the *New York Times*. Discuss the different attitudes toward story length, leads, the definition of news and design.

4) Discuss the style and effect of the following sentences:

> They told him to get lost.

> The white man's money is ice, but the land is diamonds.

> Flood out the Kakakas? Unthinkable.

5) We can discuss the structure of sentences as either cumulative or periodic. A cumulative sentence puts the subject and verb at the beginning and accumulates additional elements. Most of us write with this structure: "But the cowboy knows he is only a speck on the vast plain, his works insignificant, his power to really control the land almost nil...." The periodic structure is rare and has a decidedly different effect, as the verb or main clause is dramatically withheld until the end: "But confronted by their refusal to sell voluntarily at any price, by rising public sympathy for them and by the certainty of a lawsuit by the Indians and their environmentalist allies...the dam's proponents are caving in." Experiment with each form to learn the effect it can have on the reader.

A conversation with
William Blundell

CLARK: When people talk about good writing in American newspapers, they often mention the *Wall Street Journal*, especially those page one stories. From your point of view, as a writer and former page one editor, what is it about the stories that gives them that distinction and reputation?

BLUNDELL: I think the answer is two-pronged. One is that the *Journal*, for whatever faults it might have, has absolutely no faults in the length it will go and the time it will take to make sure the job gets done right. They are not afraid to tackle big picture stuff. They are not afraid to be imaginative, to use different forms. In fact, the page one editor, Glynn Mapes, is always encouraging people to use different forms, to try to tell different stories. They prize originality, they don't like it coming out of a can.

The other thing is the editing. You have so much attention paid to a story. The reporter will hand it in to his bureau chief and the bureau chief will go over it. He sends it to New York. The page one editor reads it, briefly, to see if he spots any real problems. If he sees no major problem it goes to a rewrite man. Then you have the final reader before it gets in the paper, generally an assistant managing editor.

I understand that on any given day, the page one editor may have 30 stories out of which he must select three, is that correct?

That varies widely. We used to run backlogs of up to 100 stories on page one, and this meant that periodically we would have the slaughter of the innocents. A lot of sub-standard stories would just go. But they don't do that any more and I think that is probably a good thing.

Many of those page one stories begin with interesting anecdotes and follow with a paragraph that captures the news in a nutshell. Is there a formula or a general sense of style that is practiced in those page one stories?

I would have to say "no" as far as a stated style is concerned. It has never been stated, to my knowledge, and I have been hanging around for 21 years. No one has ever put out a piece of paper that said this is the way we shall write our stories, or these are the values we shall have. As far as an implied style, yes, I think that is very strong. And I think that is a terrible shame.

The formula I teach is to tease the folks a little bit in the lead. They don't mind it. You are simply trying to get them interested. You are talking about a long piece now. You've got a little time. Then somewhere near the top you have to tell them what you are driving at. Then you have to show them. And along the way you do things that help them remember it. Then you try and put an ending on the story.

As far as the *Wall Street Journal* formula goes, I think a lot of young writers perceive an overly rigid formula that doesn't exist. They think you must have an anecdotal lead. You must have a certain kind of nut graph in a certain part of the story. You must do this, and you must do that.

You travel around for the *Journal*, doing some teaching and coaching in the bureaus. What sorts of writing values are you trying to communicate?

Essentially I am trying to teach them storytelling. I pay no attention to the nit-picky stuff about the meanings of words, about syntax and things like that because we are paying a lot of people very good money to sit there and clean that stuff up when it comes in. But what we are not paying them to do is tell the story for the reporter.

When I talk about storytelling, I'm talking about building the dimension of time into your story. You look at the past and you also anticipate the future. You don't just deal with the present. You go for different viewpoints. You don't have bunches of people sitting behind desks giving you the view from the left side or the right side or the view from the top. You mix it up. You always go to the action. Get down to the lowest level of where the important things in the story are happening and you detail those. You don't have other people tell us what is happening, you show them what is happening.

How would those things apply to your cowboy story for example?

One thing I am death on is the constant citation of experts which is very easy for reporters to fall into. To my way of thinking, there is no such thing as a cowboy expert. The only cowboy expert is the cowboy. And the only way you can find out and appreciate what his life is like is to work with him, and to go out with him and to be there, just hanging around. I am a tremendous believer in hanging around.

Tell me what you did at the Rafter Eleven Ranch.

I got up on a horse for the first time since I was 16 years old. Horses don't like me, and I don't like horses. This one didn't like me any better than any of the others. Fortunately, he was a hell of a lot smarter. After trying to jerk him around, you know drive up this canyon with him, Jim leaned over and said, "Why don't you just let him do what he wants to do because he is going to do it anyway."

After that, we got along pretty well, except for one bad moment when we got back down on the plain. The damn horse had this tyro up in the saddle all day long and he was just anxious to chase some cows. So the cows started to spread out when they came out of the ravine and I couldn't hold the sucker, he just bounded off after them. I was bouncing around in the saddle like a sack of meal. It is funny now, but it wasn't funny then.

How much time did you spend out there? How much time would you spend on a story like this in terms of reporting?

The key in any kind of profile is to find the right subject. I spent a week or more just finding the guy that I felt might be satisfactory, and I finally found him through a friend who is a legislator in Arizona, and a traditional rancher in traditional cattle country.

I try to define my stories in advance. I try to preconceive them if I can. I always change my mind when I get in there and start reporting. But I sat down and said I want an older man because I want to hear some stories. I don't want a young punk who doesn't have any background. I want a guy who's good because I want to show how things ought to be done. And I want a guy from traditional cattle country so I can bring in some of the flavor of the surrounding area.

I stayed at his ranch for three or four days and learned a lot about ranching. We talked over various people that he knew and everybody knows the top hand. So I called up Jim Miller and talked to him for a while and he agreed that he would put up with me for a couple of days and that's what we did.

I'm trying to visualize you flip flopping on top of a horse with a notebook in one hand. Were you able to do that?

No, you trust your memory to a certain extent when you are on horseback. You damn well better. And it is terribly rough country. I mean I was scared. But most of the information in the story, the trail ride, is just what I call a time line, it is a chronology. It is a useful device to hang the story on, it's got some action in it. But the instructive stuff and the explanatory stuff came after work. We would go down and sit around at Jim's house and he would tell me about the things we had seen, and I would blend them into the story.

That's when you were able to write things down. At some point do you sit down and recreate those moments from your memory?

Right away. Just as soon as I can. Otherwise I'll forget.

How much material would you estimate you would have collected in doing a story like this?

I would probably print about a third of what I found out.

You said that you preconceived the story in your mind. Would you plot it in any formal way?

I wouldn't necessarily have a plot, but I always try to have some sort of theme. On the cowboy story I am death on the syndrome where the reporter goes out, submits a story idea that says "a look at cowboys" or "a look at this corporation." I just think you are asking for trouble because already you know your horizon is so wide you cannot cover it all. You have to sit down and ask yourself what the hell interests you about that story, and you have to focus on those aspects. Others may pop up that are even more interesting and you have to have the flexibility to grab them. My theme for the cowboy story was how a real cowboy lives and works in an age of cowboy hype. In the lead of the story, I played off the fad and fashion of cowboys — reality vs. the illusion.

Right. You won't see John Travolta castrating any calves.

No. Not for that money, certainly.

How do you organize a piece in which you have inherently interesting information along with information that may be necessary but is less interesting?

Well, I have a set of rules that I follow and teach. They are not really rules because, as I tell the kids, if anyone sets down any hard and fast rules about writing, the last one would always be: know when to break all the others.

But generally I will try not to let two paragraphs with numbers bump against each other — ever. Because I think numbers are absolutely deadly. You try to minimize all explanation. If someone asks you what time it is, you don't tell him how to make a watch. The internal explanations of things that are going on are often pretty dull. It may be necessary, but you want to get rid of them in a hurry and get back to the action. The key thing is to keep the story moving. I never digress for more than two paragraphs from whatever my main line is. I try not to.

I notice also that those few times when the piece gets abstract, you always immediately bring it back to the concrete. To give an example, in the cowboy story where you

talk about how the cowboy knows he is only a speck on a vast plain, and Nature herself is the only manager. That is very interesting but it is abstract. You follow that with "a big buck antelope squirms."

It is really an illustration of what we are talking about. And it was suggested to me by the antelope itself. One thing that I try to teach is that the reporter belongs in the story. In every story, there are certain conclusions that any prudent man could draw from a set of facts or observations. When a reporter brings in an expert to do this he weakens his story. And there are also times when there just isn't anybody to ask and you've got to do it. That paragraph you just cited is one of those times. To me it was to say why cowboys' work is different from any other kind of work and how. And there was no one around to tell me that because the cowboys themselves don't have the basis of comparison.

And you didn't want to get the cowboy sociologist at the University of Wyoming or something to do that?

No. I'm there. I've got two eyeballs. The reader is trusting me to make informed observations and that's what I did.

Can you tell me a little bit about quotations? It seems to me that you are very demanding of your quotations. If you pick a quotation, it really contributes something new to the story, it brings something to an important conclusion, makes an abstract point human.

Why quote somebody? First of all, if you are quoting too many people in depth you get what I call "talking heads" in a story. The reporter presses a button and the head pops out of a box, waves its finger, delivers one sentence of observation or opinion, usually opinion, usually second-handed, and disappears forever.

Then you have 10, 15 of these guys in a long piece and you have just cluttered the entire thing terribly. So, first of all, I try not to quote anybody that is only going to get in the way of my story. And only quote those people who are centrally involved or have something very sharp to say.

And then, do you have any feelings about whether you quote briefly or at length?

I prefer to quote briefly. I mean if you've got a Winston Churchill on your hands, I think I'd quote him at length. Most people aren't Winston Churchill. And who's the writer here anyway? You are. If the guy is just blathering on and on, I think you tighten the screws down on his quote till you get the essence out of it. Sometimes, if you need him in the story, if his credibility is important, you've got to have him, but he has never said an interesting thing in his life and you just paraphrase him with some zip.

I notice that you tend to place quotes, not always, but in many instances, at the ends of paragraphs, and on a couple of occasions at the end of the story as well. What does that do for you?

No real system designed that. I try to teach reporters that if they have an important point they want to make, make it repetitiously but in different ways. Make it with a figure, make it with an anecdote, and then maybe wrap it up with a quote.

I would like to talk a little bit about endings. I think traditionally journalism is so top heavy that people spend a lot of time thinking about the beginnings of their stories but hardly ever think about the end.

That is so right. I am very hip on endings. You have punched the red button now.

OK. Why don't you talk to me about endings.

Well, first of all I lament the lack of any decent ending in a lot of stories that appear in most newspapers, and also in the *Wall Street Journal*. The story just bleeds away and what a shame. If you've gotten the guy to read down that far, it seems to me that what you want to do is nail it into his consciousness.

When we talked about the dimension in time, a lot of the endings that I try and put on stories have to do with the future. What's going to happen next? And I don't rely on scholarly studies for that. Ask the people who are right there. What do they think? Sometimes you can get something provocative. Another good ending is to circle around the central meaning of your story, but do it in a different way. The circle reminds the reader of the main theme at the very end.

One thing I noticed about your ending on Jim Miller's story is that you give a sense of completion and closure for the reader without the sort of flashing lights that sometime accompany artificial codas, if you know what I mean. In other words you have ended at a point where the story seems to be over, which seems like the natural place.

Yes. I wish there were some formula to apply to that, but I don't think there is. If you sit down in front of the typewriter and say now I will end my story with a flash of adjectives and a swizzle of power verbs, I don't think it is going to work. It is going to look artificial and tacked on. I think the story dictates what its own end should be. And you just know it when you write it. You say that's enough. That is going to satisfy.

Permit me to stereotype the readers of the *Journal* for a moment. I associate them with the business ethic, with the values of growth, progress, development, new technology. Your stories here are about cultures which reflect different values: cowboys, loggers, Indians. What is your reaction to that observation?

In the job that I have now, I think I do two things mostly. I deal with resource issues because the *Journal* and every other publication that I know of is doing a crappy job on what goes into the pipeline. And as far as business coverage is concerned, they are all over what comes out of the end: the shipping of it, the financing of it, the corporate structures involved with it, that sort of thing. But we are paying very little attention to central resource issues and most of those are in the West. That is number one.

Number two is I am in the business of introducing Americans to each other because we take each other disgracefully for granted and yet we depend on each other in an urban society to a degree that is breathtaking. Go down to Safeway and, for all most people know, the lettuce grew right out of the produce bins. So in doing a story like Loggers, for example, I want people to know that when they go down to the lumber yard to build some bookshelves there might be a little bit of blood on those boards.

Tell me about the reporting of the loggers story.

One thing I didn't do was cut down a tree. I can tell you that. Too damn dangerous. I think it would have violated their safety rules, and I try to play by the rules if I can.

Let me pose this problem for you. In the case of the cowboys, the Indians, and loggers, what was their reaction to a reporter

from the *Wall Street Journal*. We think of some of those societies, the cowboy society, being essentially non-verbal, I mean in terms of our stereotypes anyway.

That's true. It's very true. Cowboys say little.

Did that pose any particular interviewing problems for you? What sort of questions and attitudes do you have to adopt in order to get these people to talk to you?

If you go in there with a laundry list of questions, and you've got blinkers on, and you don't observe what's going on, you really are going to miss the guts of the story. You keep your eyes open and as far as relating to people is concerned, I hate the laundry list approach. Sometimes I'll use it if all I'm interested in is a factual response. But most of the time I'm interested in an emotional response and I'm trying, even in the half-hour interview, to get a little closer to this guy than might ordinarily be possible.

I usually do that by showing real interest in what he does for a living. And I am interested in what he does for a living, so I guess it shows. Most of the loggers are reading the funny papers up there. They never read the *Wall Street Journal*. Their image of the *Wall Street Journal* is completely out of whack, and so they are all wondering what the hell I am doing there.

So this one cutter looks up at me and says "Oh, he's come to do a story about us crazy tree fallers." I said, "Blundell, you are in trouble, you're in heavy trouble, just keep your mouth shut and watch the guy work." After a couple of innocuous questions, I spent about three hours watching him work. At lunch he began talking about how he felt about his work. That is the story really. How you feel about it, not the mechanics of what you do.

Did you have any sense of what this logger story would be like? Our stereotype of what loggers do is kind of eating pancakes or wearing flannel shirts or something like that. Did you have any sense of that?

No. I didn't. What was interesting to me about that story was the tremendous danger quotient in logging, and I reasoned before I ever went in, this would have to do something to the people who did it. I was looking for the differences between loggers and everybody else. I was looking for the characteristics of loggers as workers and as working men. That's what I focused on. The idea of fraternity just popped up when I got back with all of the material. I looked at it and I said "Gee, they haze people, they blackball people, they don't allow women. What are these guys, a fraternity would you say?"

You haven't talked too much about your actual writing habits.

Before I sit down in front of the keyboard, I do two things. I read this whole pile of stuff quickly. I am talking about a major story now. And I will cull the stuff that seems dull or repetitive or a little bit off my subject.

This leaves me with a working pile. And then I use a six-point outline for every story. It is not even an outline. I categorize my material. A few of these things are of interest, and others may not be, but I always consider all six of them. 1) I deal with history. 2) I deal with scope, what I am talking about. 3) I deal with the central reasons behind what is going on, political, economic, and social. 4) I deal with impacts, who's helped or hurt by this, and to what extent, and what's their emotional response to it? 5) I deal with the gathering and action of *contrary forces*. If this is going on, is somebody trying to do anything about it, and how is that working out? 6) And at the very end I will deal with the future.

If this stuff keeps up, what are things going to look like five or ten years from now, in the eyes of the people who are directly involved?

Rather than being a structure for writing, this is a sort of a frame of reference for the information you've collected.

Say I've got 20 interviews on a story, which wouldn't be unusual. I will number all of those. I'd use "T" for Interviews, T-1 through 20. Under those outline headings I gave you, I'll start plugging in material. The outline consists of three or four sheets of yellow paper stapled together with these headings.

I will put, say "T-1Q Goddamn bums" that means in the first of those interviews, the source is giving a quote (Q) that has a bearing on history and the words that I use simply are a reminder of what he said.

I go through all of that material that way, and I will segregate that stuff, and it doesn't take all that long. And then I write off that. I don't bother to look through the pile. I only plug in the actual specifics at the end.

So you begin writing without your notes.

I'm writing without my notes because I don't want to have to stop if I'm cooking real well. I don't want to have to stop and go through piles of paper.

Do you have to find your lead before you can proceed?

No. What I teach people to do is work on their main theme, work on it throughout the reporting until they've got it, a clear exposition, almost ready-made to drop somewhere into the story. And then, if they are stuck for a lead, if they are stuck for a half-hour or something like that, start writing the expository part of the story. That's the easy part to write.

The lead comes from the right side of the brain, bubbles up through there. The writer sits down and rolls it in his typewriter and sits there and is literally saying OK now be creative. I think you can push around the left side of your brain. You can say be logical, but you can't push around the right side.

At that point, in most cases will you just try to get a decent first draft under your belt?

I never write more than a first draft. After I go through this stuff, while I am indexing it all and putting it into categories, I'm also thinking about story line. I tell the story chronologically, I use a time line, and I use a theme line, and I use a cause and effect line.

There are other certain common sub-sections that I can deal with. For example, in Cowboy there is one section where the guy ropes a calf and he talks about how in real life it is almost never done in cowboying. It is done in rodeo but it's not done in cowboying, and the guy who has to do it all the time is a crappy cowboy. This launches you into a whole natural section on cattle handling, so I pick out all of my cattle handling stuff that I find interesting and lay it down in one place.

When you say that you never write more than one draft, you are talking about your building the piece as you progress, so that when you reach the end it is pretty much done?

Yes, probably a little too long, but then I go through a very rigorous self-editing process.

Tell me about that a little bit. What sort of things are you looking for?

Well, the first thing I do, is make the story

longer. I'll take a look at the main points of my story. I ask myself "Have I left something out that would be an added convincer?" And so I will go back to the notes and put it in sometimes.

After that, I will sort of turn the process upside down. I think most reporters are looking for big hunks to cut out at first. The first thing I do is go word by word and I question every word I have written. Usually I can cut little extra phrases and words that don't add anything at all to the story. I get rid of all the Siamese twins, you know the double sentences. I combine them into one and by the time I am through, I've usually got a take out of the story without missing a damn thing.

I will look at the secondary points and I will try and generalize some of them if I still need to save some space. Only then will I attack the main sections of the story. If that's the blood and bone, I don't want to cut it if I can help it.

Bill, that covers most of my territory. Can you think of anything else about your writing, about these stories, that I may have overlooked, that you would like to talk about?

Maybe just a general principle and it has nothing to do necessarily with me or my particular work. It is just that I have the sort of assignment where it is imperative to go down on the ground all the time, and to go to the lowest level of what has happened. There are very few massive studies, very few think tankers, there are very few bureaucrats who can really talk to me about the things that I report. I think the character of reporters has changed to the point where, instead of being lower level Irish sons of Irish saloon keepers, we now have a brie and chablis image. A lot of the reporters are very comfortable. They are upper middle class to upper class people. They are well educated, and they tend to move more easily with the desk people and movers and shakers and bureaucrats. But I think they are losing the ability to get down and roll around in the dirt at the level where the action is. Instead, we are hanging around in think tanks and the ante-rooms of politicians, perhaps more than we should be. Sure, we've got to be there. You have to be out on the street, too.

Patrick Sloyan
Deadline Writing

PATRICK J. SLOYAN, 45, covers Europe and the Mideast for the Long Island newspaper *Newsday* which he joined in 1974 after serving 14 years in the Washington bureaus of United Press International and the Hearst newspapers. He has lived in London since 1981, heading the *Newsday* bureau there. Born in Stamford, Connecticut, Sloyan grew up in several U.S. cities and spent a year in Italy. At 18, he enlisted in the Army and became involved in journalism "primarily because I could type." After the Army, he graduated from the University of Maryland and worked part time for the *Baltimore News American* before joining UPI in Washington.

Anwar Sadat assassinated at Cairo military review

OCTOBER 7, 1981

CAIRO — Egyptian President Anwar Sadat, a modern-day pharaoh who attempted to lead the Arab world toward a permanent Mideast peace with Israel, was assassinated yesterday by a band of soldiers who attacked a military parade reviewing stand with automatic rifles and hand grenades.

The 62-year-old Sadat, who had been laughing heartily only moments before, was mortally wounded by a bullet and a grenade fragment. An official medical bulletin later said, "There were two holes in the left side of the chest, a bullet in the neck just above the right collarbone, a wound above the right knee, a huge gash at the back of the left thigh and a complicated fracture of the thigh...(death was attributed to) violent nervous shock, and internal bleeding in the chest cavity, where the left lung and major blood vessels below it were torn."

Seven other persons were killed and 22 were wounded, including four Americans.

Sadat's death further jeopardized hopes of a lasting Mideast peace that has been stalemated for more than two years. Nevertheless, Sadat's hand-picked successor, Vice President Hosni Mubarak, 52, was expected to continue the same domestic and foreign policies. Like Sadat, Mubarak has the strong backing of the Egyptian military. It was Mubarak who announced Sadat's death to the nation in a dramatic television appearance seven hours after the incident. He declared a year-long state of emergency.

According to Egyptian army officials, an army lieutenant and four enlisted men staged the attack that transformed a hot, sunny day of military muscle-flexing into a nightmare for thousands crowded into a massive concrete stadium. The attackers shouted, "Glory to Egypt! Attack! You are agents! You are intruders!" at the large crowd of dignitaries.

At least one of the attackers was killed by police and four others were reported to be under arrest. Military sources said the attackers were either Moslem fanatics or backers of a former Egyptian chief of staff, Lt. Gen. Saad Eddin El-Shazli, who broke with Sadat over the peace treaty with Israel and is now in exile in Lebanon.

The parade was a grand show with both American and older Soviet hardware on display. No one enjoyed it more than Sadat, who smiled and laughed noisily for the watching press corps. Paratroopers had just successfully landed within a few feet of Sadat who was sitting behind a railing in the front row of the reviewing stand. All eyes turned upwards as six Egyptian Mirage jets roared over the reviewing stand, pulling up sharply in acrobatic rolls and turns that left plumes of red, white, blue and yellow smoke in their wake. It was just then — 12:40 p.m. local time (6:40 a.m. EDT) — that Associated Press photographer William Foley said, "All hell broke loose."

From a truck towing an artillery piece in the parade, a group of soldiers — one of them bare-headed — began firing what appeared, from photographs, to be Soviet-made AK-47 automatic rifles. "I thought it was part of the show at first," said AP reporter Steve Hindy. One of the soldiers jumped from the truck and lobbed a grenade at the reviewing stand. Others joined him. They held their rifles to their shoulders and, blazing away, began running toward the reviewing stand. A second grenade was thrown. One rifleman walked right up to the railing within four feet of Sadat and sprayed the reviewing stand. Eyewitnesses said the gunfire lasted at least a minute.

It took that long for the crowd to react.

Those on the VIP platform tumbled from their chairs to the floor. Screaming and shouting erupted, and panic seized the crowd that began to flee in all directions. Many of them fell over one another; bodies littered the ground. Security guards or police — no one is sure — began firing, felling one of the attackers.

According to one government source, Sadat was unconscious moments after being wounded. He was flown from the site by helicopter to Maadi Military Hospital and arrived at 1:20 p.m. local time. Doctors said he was in a coma when he arrived. Sadat was finally pronounced dead at 2:40 p.m.

Sadat's wife, Jihan, had watched the parade from a box just above the reviewing stand. At the hospital, a doctor, his face streaming with tears, broke the news to her, saying, "Only God is immortal." Mrs. Sadat collapsed in tears, witnesses said.

Back at the reviewing stand, it was a blood-spattered and grisly scene. Shot dead were Sadat's personal secretary, Fawzi Abdel Hafez; official photographer, Mohamed Rashwan; chief chamberlain Hassan Allam, a security guard and one still unidentified man.

Ambulances evacuated the wounded, who included Americans Richard McCleskey of Raytheon Corp.; Air Force Capt. Christopher Ryan; Marine Maj. Jerald Agenbroad of the U.S. Rapid Deployment Office; and Air Force Lt. Col. Charles D. Loney from the Defense Department in Washington.

In addition to the four Americans, the wounded reportedly included eight Egyptians; the Belgian ambassador, Claude Ruelle; and the Irish defense minister, James Tully. One of the Egyptians was Bishop Samuel, whom Sadat had appointed last month to a committee replacing Pope Shenuda III as patriarch of the Christian Coptic church. Some reports said Samuel was dead.

Early today, Cairo was quiet. There was no

hint of a further move against the government. Noticeably absent was any sign of public mourning for Sadat, who has been criticized in recent months for his crackdown on political opponents. By contrast, Cairo's streets were jammed with literally millions of weeping Egyptians when Gamal Abdel Nasser died suddenly of a heart attack on Sept. 28, 1970. Those crowds only disbanded when a false report of an attack on Cairo was circulated. The next day, seven million people gathered again to mourn the loss of their leader.

Sadat assumed power on Oct. 15, 1970, and led Egypt through the 1972 break in diplomatic relations with the Soviet Union, the 1973 Yom Kippur War with Israel, and finally to Camp David in Maryland in 1978 for a peace treaty with Israeli Prime Minister Menachem Begin and former President Jimmy Carter.

Sadat's death was a blow to the U.S. and Israel — and, some experts fear, to the cause of peace in the Middle East. President Reagan denounced the assassination as an act of "cowardly infamy" and lauded Sadat as a "courageous man whose vision and wisdom brought nations and people together."

The gravity of the situation was underlined by Secretary of State Alexander Haig, who called all senators to a briefing at 5 p.m. in the Capitol. Senators who attended the closed meeting said Haig suggested that there might have been some Libyan involvement in the assassination.

Administration officials said that elements of the U.S. Rapid Deployment Force and U.S. warships in the Mediterranean "have been placed on increased readiness" as means of warning Libyan leader Moammar Khadafy not to take advantage of the situation in Egypt.

Israeli Prime Minister Menachem Begin said the Egyptian president had been "murdered by the enemies of peace." Begin referred to Sadat's commitment to the Camp David accord worked out under the supervision of former

President Jimmy Carter. "It was a difficult road," Begin said in a prepared statement. "Unforgettable are the days of Camp David. So is the hour in which the president of Egypt and the prime minister of Israel signed a treaty of peace between our two countries and the president of the United States attached his signature as a witness to that historic act."

Pope John Paul II also expressed his sorrow. "In condemning this treacherous act of violence, I pray that almighty God may grant peace to this man of peace and bring to fulfillment his lofty vision of reconciliation among peoples."

Not surprisingly, the response of the Soviet Union was far different. The government-run radio quoted "analysts" as saying that the attack stemmed from the "discontent of Egyptians with Sadat's foreign and domestic policies, especially the peace treaty with the Israeli aggressor and military cooperation with the United States." The report was the last news item. A sports update followed.

Sadat was the driving force and chief architect of the treaty with Israel. But most of his Arab neighbors opposed the move, and many Arab nations rejoiced at word of his death. There was dancing in the streets of Tripoli, Libya's capital. "Camp David killed Sadat," was the way Lebanese President Shafik Wazzan summed up Arab sentiment.

Just before the assassination, Sadat was surrounded by members of his staff, the diplomatic corps and Christian and Moslem clergymen at the military show in Nasser, a suburb between the city airport and downtown Cairo. They sweltered in the 95-degree sunshine. Thousands of soldiers passed in review at the ceremony that marked Egypt's 1973 attack on Israel.

Sadat's fate was kept from the Egyptian people for hours. Cairo radio played a steady stream of patriotic music. At one point, officials confirmed Sadat had been wounded, but only slightly in the arm.

Alfred Atherton, U.S. Ambassador to Egypt, was on the reviewing stand but escaped unhurt. Initially, Atherton wired the State Department that Sadat was safe.

After Sadat's death, Mubarak called an emergency session of the cabinet to inform the ministers. It was after that meeting that Mansour Hassan, the deputy speaker of the Parliament, confirmed to waiting reporters that Sadat had died. But most of Egypt did not get the news until Mubarak's televised announcement. Throughout the night, Cairo radio played readings from the Koran. Government officials said Sadat's funeral would be held either on tomorrow or Saturday, with Saturday the most likely. Leaders from around the world were expected to attend.

Technically, Egypt is under the control of a provisional president, Sufi Hassan Abu Taled, speaker of the parliament. But the power clearly rested in the hands of Mubarak, a former Air Force pilot whom Sadat had been grooming as his successor.

(According to former President Jimmy Carter, Sadat was ready to quit. "He told me he was going to step down next year," said Carter in a telephone interview from Plains, Ga. Carter met with Sadat a few weeks ago after the Egyptian president had visited Washington.)

Observations and questions

1) Sloyan selects each word in his lead with care. No word is wasted. He also uses sentence structure, word order, verb form and subordination to create meaning and emphasis for the reader:

   A) He begins with Sadat's name as subject, placing full emphasis on the tragic figure of the Egyptian president.

   B) He follows with the phrase "a modern-day pharaoh" in apposition. In so doing he uses the connotations of the word to give his lead a historical center of gravity. The connotations of *pharaoh* are at least twofold: a great, almost divine leader who builds a civilization in the desert; and someone who has enslaved and persecuted the people of Israel. The lead supports the first connotation and plays off the second.

   C) A relative clause "who attempted to lead the Arab world..." places Sadat in a historical context and hints at what made him an object of hatred.

   D) The verb *was assassinated* is the turning point in the lead. It is the news, of course. Although writers prefer the active voice, they sometimes use the passive voice to give full attention to the receiver of the action — in this case, Sadat.

   E) The verb turns the lead to the shocking violence of the news event. Sloyan brings that violence home by ending his lead with the words "automatic rifles and hand grenades." Their placement at the end of the paragraph gives them special emphasis.

2) Sloyan's story is a good example of journalism as "instant history." How does the writer create a sense of history in this piece? What sets it apart, in terms of authority and gravity, from more routine pieces?

3) Examine the first six paragraphs of Sloyan's story. Each paragraph answers at least one important question for the reader. What are these questions? Discuss the order of these paragraphs. Can you think of a different, more appropriate order?

4) Notice how Sloyan balances traditional news values with the demands of narrative. Sloyan places the important information high in the story, stacking the news in the first six paragraphs. But the seventh paragraph, "The parade was a grand show," begins a chronological narrative of the event in high dramatic fashion.

5) Sloyan accomplished this story under extraordinary deadline pressure. He considered any source of information available to him. Carefully reread the story and examine the sources of Sloyan's information. Also consider the reliability of those sources and the process of verification and attribution employed by the reporter.

6) Sloyan's eighth paragraph reveals the special effectiveness of the active voice in recounting narrative events. Read that paragraph aloud and discuss his use of verbs.

Sadat is entombed as world pays tribute

OCTOBER 10, 1981

CAIRO — "Look," said Richard M. Nixon to Jimmy Carter.

"What?" said Carter.

"Look, just above the eagle — see the bullet holes," said Nixon. "And look at the ceiling — those are bullet holes, too."

Gerald R. Ford started to gape also.

The three former presidents of the United States were caught yesterday in a crush at the funeral of Anwar Sadat that was getting out of hand. A line of march of more than a thousand — sweating princes, prime ministers, generals, reporters and friends of the family — had converged on a bottleneck.

It was beneath the cantilevered concrete roof where Sadat sat Tuesday when he was riddled by bullets by a band of fanatic Moslems. The roadblock was a small glass door at the rear of what serves as a military parade reviewing stand. On the other side of the door was the widow, Jihan Sadat, and the receiving line.

"Make way for Prince Charles," shouted a man with an Arabic accent. Nixon, Ford and Carter stepped to one side and then were moved even further as security forces from a dozen nations shoved and pushed to get their dignitaries through the glass doors.

Nixon was the first to spot the aftermath of the assassination: four bullet holes in the ceiling and chunks of marble missing from a massive backdrop that included a huge golden eagle. Twenty feet from where they stood, blood dried brown stained a white wall. Even so, it was cleaner than it was on Friday, when even a casual passerby at the stadium in Nasser City could find an invitation to the Tuesday parade stuck to the platform by congealed blood.

There were more than blood stains and bullet holes to remind the dignitaries of what had happened at the stadium. The Egyptian chief of staff showed up with a bandage on his cheekbone, which had been grazed by a bullet. He was sitting immediately to Sadat's left when the shooting started.

For some diplomats, it was an upsetting return. "Why the hell did they bring us back here?" said one Australian diplomat. That embassy's deputy chief, John Woods, had been wounded in the gunfire with a bullet that struck his lung and liver. He was one of more than a dozen members of the diplomatic corps who were caught by bursting grenades and machine gun fire on Tuesday.

To the rear, near the pyramid-shaped tomb of the Egyptian Unknown Soldier, Sadat's body lay in the Cairo sun. By then, no one was looking at his casket on the caisson drawn by six black horses that had become motionless in the heat. Only their tails moved to chase the swarming flies. The state funeral had turned into one of those noisy wakes where, for the moment, the corpse was forgotten.

Three ranks of security personnel — white-uniformed police soldiers in red berets and a blue-helmeted force with machine guns that seemed to be keeping watch on the soldiers — flanked the world delegation. Thousands of guards — the government had no exact count — had sealed the Cairo suburb from thousands of Egyptian citizens. Police used 12-foot bamboo rods to beat back one mob in a dusty encounter a mile from the procession. Egyptian helicopters hovered nearby.

The funeral started just before noon with a roll of drums and a blast of trumpets. Mrs. Sadat, Rosalynn Carter and other women in the delegations were taken to the reviewing stand by limousines before the procession began.

It ended two hours later after Sadat was

laid in his grave, which bore the inscription, "Thou shalt not count those who were killed for the sake of God as dead, for they are alive with God." He was buried less than 50 yards from where he was mortally wounded.

Sadat's caisson was preceded by a mounted officer, and three soldiers were mounted on three of the horses pulling the caisson. His casket was covered with a red and white silk flag with a golden eagle — the symbol of Egypt — in the center.

Earlier in the day his body had been flown from Maadi Hospital to the parade ground. It was the reverse of the trip on Tuesday when he arrived at the hospital by helicopter with five wounds and blood seeping through his lips.

While Sadat's children held their heads in the air, his wife wept. Saluting cannons and rifle fire echoed in the stadium.

When the horde of official delegates were signaled to assemble on the parade line, there was an undiplomatic rush to get up front, just behind the male part of Sadat's family that followed the caisson.

Lost in the shuffle was French President Francois Mitterrand. "Mitterrand, Mitterrand," someone called from the front of the line of march.

Israeli Prime Minister Menachem Begin, who is 5-feet-8, was lost in a sea of burly bodyguards in yarmulkes who elbowed other world leaders aside to protect their leader.

Carter got separated from the other former presidents for a time. The Africans, the Indians, the Italians all jockeyed for frontline positions. Soon they made up the vanguard of the procession as the Americans fell back.

Off to one side was the British delegation, almost aloof from the others. Prince Charles seemed the only man on the parade ground who was cool and dry. He was in Navy whites that reflected the 90-degree sun. A pale blue sash was draped from his left shoulder. He carried a gold sword in his right hand.

Begin had joined the Americans. So had former French President Valery Giscard d'Estaing, who towered over the Israeli leader and Carter. Nixon and Henry Kissinger stuck together. "Keep cool," Nixon had warned before the procession. "I was at the shah's funeral here and it was hot as hell."

Plodding along in the American delegation was its youngest official member, 14-year-old Sam Brown of Liberty, S.C.

His pen-pal relationship with Sadat had won him an invitation to Egypt in 1979, when Brown was only 12. It was Sam's biggest day, he said, since the South Carolina band competition. He plays the drums. Sam was wearing a $90 suit that Liberty businessmen helped him pay for.

He said he was taking home two bottles of Pepsi-Cola and two bottles of 7-Up — both lettered in Arabic. "I'm going to sell two and keep the others because I think they're valuable," he said.

About 15 minutes after the procession started, and just as the vanguard neared the reviewing stand where the assassination had taken place, there was a sudden scare.

A line of guards — the ones in the blue helmets with machine guns — suddenly ran in front of the marchers, blocking their way. For a few seconds, the delegates veered in panic. But then the soldiers were moved out of the way by a barking Egyptian officer in gold braid.

A French government official, his black wool suit making the heat even worse, paled for a moment. "I do not know where is my President," he said, anxiously. Quickly, the fears subsided.

The drums continued to roll and on they marched in the dust.

"Where is the assassination site?" asked Carter.

"Right ahead, Mr. President," answered

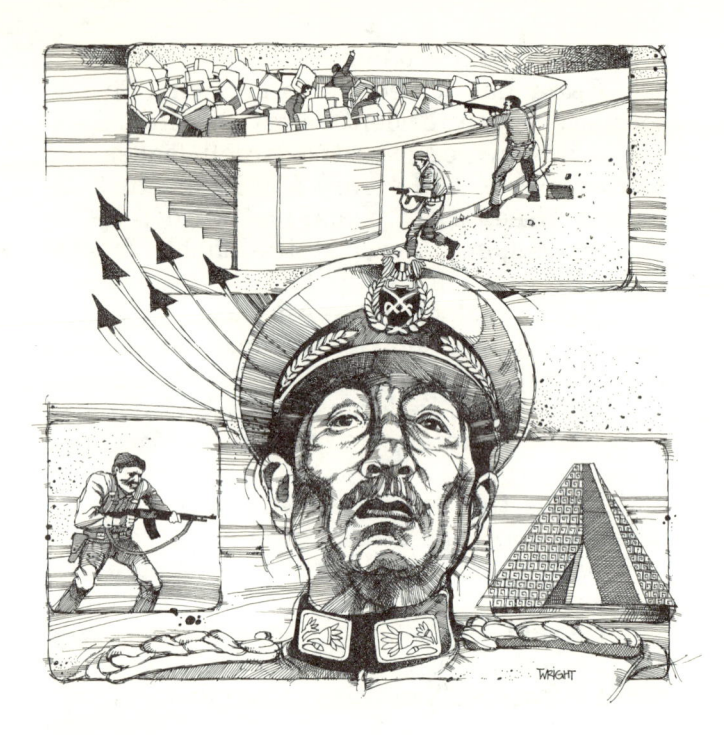

Ashraf Ghorbal, the Egyptian ambassador to Washington. The site where Sadat had fallen had become a jam of humanity and shouting security guards.

The American delegation veered away, circled up the steps and came to a halt outside the glass doors at the rear of the reviewing stand.

"I don't think we're going to be able to get through there," said Carter.

"No," agreed Nixon.

Ford swung the massive shoulders that once made him an all-American lineman at Michigan to get a little closer. But then he retreated. "I guess you're right," Ford said to Carter.

It was then that Nixon pointed out the bullet holes. They watched a small stout Indian diplomat lower his head and barrel through the doorway, knocking aside soldiers and security guards.

A Secret Service agent didn't like the looks of the mob scene. "We're not coming in there until the room clears," the agent told the guards at the door. Soon it was cleared and the Americans paid their respects to Mrs. Sadat.

"We love you, and we love your family," said House Majority Leader Jim Wright (D-Texas), after kissing Mrs. Sadat's hand.

The Americans and most of the other delegations had left Nasser City by the time the final ceremony began. The only one who stayed with the family was President Gaafar Nemeiri of Sudan, who has aligned his desert nation with Egypt. Nemeiri was one of the few Arab leaders at the funeral, reflecting Sadat's isolation from most of the Arab world.

"In the name of God almighty, the merciful, the God we worship," sang the Moslem priest in opening the service. He read the portion of the Koran designed to relieve the soul of its earthly burdens and help Sadat in his judgment by God.

A marble slab was removed at the base of the unknown soldier's tomb. An honor guard removed the casket and took it to the grave. There it was eased into the crypt by Sadat's son, Gamal, and his brothers, Ismat and Talaak, following Moslem custom.

A mausoleum in Sadat's memory will be erected nearby. But it was the marble grave cover that bore the words he wanted — "He lived for peace and died for principles."

After the funeral, most of the American delegation, including Ford and Carter, boarded Air Force One for the trip home.

Haig stayed behind for meetings with Begin, Egyptian leaders and representatives of Somalia, Oman, Sudan and Liberia. State Department spokesmen Dean Fischer said the officials agreed on the need to defend the Mideast and Africa against intervention.

"There was agreement in the meetings on the need to defend the region against external intervention or internal intervention manipulated by outside forces," Fischer said.

His statement apparently referred to Libya,

which has tried to recruit an invasion force of Sudanese exiles to attack their homeland. Fischer said Haig and Begin shared the view that there would be continuity in Egypt, that the transition would be smooth and that the government is competent to handle the situation.

Nixon slipped into Saudi Arabia Saturday night. He had been scheduled to return with the rest of the delegation, but it wasn't until after the presidential aircraft left Cairo that State Department officials got queries about Nixon's location.

"Mr. Nixon went to Saudi Arabia," said an assistant to Haig. "We had no idea he was going. He didn't tell anyone."

(In Washington, a White House spokesman said Nixon's trip was private and that he was not carrying any messages from Reagan. He is also planning to go to Jordan, Tunisia, and Morocco, the spokesman said.)

(The Saudi state radio said Nixon met with King Khaled and later had dinner with him and Crown Prince Fahd. Fischer said Nixon was not on a mission for Haig connected with the proposed AWACS radar aircraft sale to the Saudis.)

Saudi Arabia was among the countries that boycotted the funeral. Some of the radical regimes condemned Arabs who attended, partly because of the presence of Begin and partly because of their dislike of Sadat.

Syria's state-run radio proclaimed "The traitor is buried forever" and Tripoli Radio said that those who "walked behind his dirty corpse were a bunch of imperialist traitors."

Meanwhile, Lt. Gen. Saadeddin Sgazli, an opposition leader in exile in Tripoli, called on Egyptians to boycott Tuesday's referendum on the choice of Hosni Mubarak to succeed Sadat.

Criticizing Mubarak for pledging to continue Sadat's policies, he said that if the referendum took place, "violence is the only answer."

Observations and questions

1) A reporter rarely begins any story, especially a breaking news story, with dialogue. Discuss the opening of this story. Consider how Sloyan uses the opening scene and dialogue as a focus for recounting Sadat's funeral.

2) Clearly, the writer portrays political leaders and heads of state as human beings rather than as simple figures of authority. In fact, the event strips them of some of their grandeur. Look at Sloyan's description and characterization of former Presidents Nixon, Ford and Carter. To what extent do these correspond to their public images? Are there any surprises?

3) What does the anecdote about 12-year-old Sam Brown add to the story?

4) The writer uses more description of people and places in this story than in the previous one. Here, of course, Sloyan is an eyewitness. Look at the details of description — the uniform of Prince Charles, for example. Try to read the author's mind. Why does he select certain elements of description? How do they contribute to the story?

5) Are you surprised at the chaos, lack of discipline and disorganization of this event? Hasn't Sloyan created, intentionally or not, a story which serves as a microcosm of a society that is out of joint?

6) Compare and contrast Sloyan's accounts of these events with similar accounts in other newspapers. Discuss the strengths and weaknesses of the different approaches to the story.

Assassination plot traced to Islamic defiance

OCTOBER 12, 1981

CAIRO — It began at a barber shop in a dusty town along the Suez Canal with two young soldiers who had defied the Egyptian army edict to shave every morning. They were marched to the artillery base barber and were ordered to have removed the stubble of a day's growth. When they refused they were dismissed from the army on the spot.

A young lieutenant in the unit based only 20 miles from Cairo was sympathetic to the two young recruits. Mohammed, the Prophet of Allah, wore a beard. It was the mark of a true believer. The refusal to permit beards was another example of those who do not govern by the law of Allah. There must be a retreat from these Western ways, and those responsible for what is wrong with Egypt must be killed.

According to western intelligence officials, the time was 1979 and the young lieutenant was Khaled Ahmed Shawki El Eslambuly. The incident is one important nugget of evidence obtained by Egyptian investigators frantically tracing the origins of the plot to assassinate President Anwar Sadat on Oct. 6.

Those three men, along with a last-minute addition, carried out the carefully planned attack on a military parade reviewing stand that left Sadat mortally wounded, at least eight others dead, and more than 30 bleeding. It was a machine gun, rifle and grenade assault staged just as it is drawn up in the Egyptian infantry handbook. Within 23 seconds, stability in the Mideast was severely shaken.

The plot may have had even deeper roots than the 1979 incident. In 1974 Khaled's brother was among a band that staged a bloody attack on an Egyptian military academy where Sadat had been scheduled to speak. He was imprisoned for that attack, and he also was among those arrested last month in Sadat's crackdown on Moslem dissidents. Western officials say Egyptian investigators suspect the man was part of the successful plot to assassinate Sadat. Khaled and his brother were both members of a secret society, the Takfir Wahigra. It is a subgroup of the Moslem Brotherhood and, like 40 other such cells, it has its own special version of what Egyptian society should be to please Allah.

Western sources say Egyptian investigators believe that when Khaled's brother was jailed, it forced the plotters to get a new man at the last moment. In public statements by Egyptian officials since the assassination, only a partial picture of events has emerged. Khaled was in command of a three-ton Soviet truck that would tow a Soviet-made 130mm artillery piece — a fragment of thousands of troops who practiced for days to get the 10-mile parade organized and on schedule. The rehearsals also permitted Khaled to time his attack from that truck perfectly.

Khaled had told his superiors that three of his regular artillery men were ill and would be unable to make the parade. But he said he had three other soldiers who would perch precisely on seats in the bed of the truck for the parade. The government stressed that the substitutes were all civilians — the two men who wanted to grow beards and a third who was formerly on active duty but at the time held status only as a reserve officer. Their uniforms were obtained by Khaled. Army rules prohibit anyone from carrying live ammunition in the parade, an annual event to celebrate Egypt's attack on Israel in the so-called Yom Kippur War of 1973 — a traditional "Victory Day" celebration. According to the government, bullets, fragmentation and concussion grenades were obtained outside of the armed forces from a still-unidentified source in "Upper Egypt." This usually means Assyut, where illegal activities in everything from gun-running to dope-smuggling flourish. It is also the city where more than 100 died in an attack on police last week by Moslem fundamentalists two days after Sadat's death.

Khaled arrived with the ammunition at the parade staging ground in Nasser City about 4:30 a.m. Government officials say the evidence so far indicates four other men in the truck — three on the bed and the driver — were not involved in the plot. The men got in their truck and waited for their turn to pass before the reviewing stand.

Sadat stepped out of a black Cadillac at about 11 a.m. The sun glared in the bright blue sky. The temperature was already in the 90s. There was a noticeable gasp of appreciation among Egyptians already beneath the cantilevered concrete roof of the grandstand. It was caused by Sadat's new uniform — navy blue with a dark green sash across his breast along with a four-inch row of medals. Gleaming leather boots reached almost to his kneecaps. Gold braid on his shoulders and his hat glinted in the sunlight.

Opening ceremonies included a speech thanking the United States for new M-60 tanks that would be on display for the first time in the parade that day. Sadat also placed a wreath at the Tomb of the Unknown Soldier, about 50 yards from the reviewing stand. He moved gracefully with the wreath, putting it gently on a spot beneath the soaring pyramid-shaped tomb. He would be buried on that same spot four days later.

Back at the reviewing stand, he removed his hat, lit his pipe and sat back to enjoy the show. He chatted, smiled and laughed with Vice President Hosni Mubarak who, as always, was at Sadat's right side. On Sadat's left was Lt. Gen. Abb Rabul Nabi Hafez, Army chief of staff.

It was a splendid show, including everything from cavalry on prancing Arabian stallions and undulating camels to a free-fall parachuting display that had Sadat clapping as the paratroopers in their red, white and blue chutes landed within a few feet of the grandstand.

There was an embarrassing moment at one point, particularly with all the diplomats watching. First a motorcycle and then a jeep stalled in the parade line and had to be pushed out of the way. But it was soon forgotten when the Egyptian Air Force roared onto the scene. Groups of F-4 Phantoms, Soviet MiGs and French Mirages took turns dazzling the crowd. All trailed red, yellow, blue and white smoke, plumes that tracked the trajectories of the jet fighters. Few were looking at the parade column only 20 meters away from the reviewing stand. A relatively boring line of sand-colored artillery trucks was moving by at eight miles an hour. By contrast, six Mirages swooped in at 12:40 p.m. at 200 feet then pulled steeply into an aerobatic climb. Everyone, including the television cameraman, followed the flight, even Sadat's blue-bereted paratroop unit that makes up his elite bodyguard.

"They were only human," said Ossama El Baz, a Sadat aide who defended the bodyguards later.

Inside the truck, Lt. Khaled pointed his machine gun at the driver and told him to stop or be killed. When the driver hesitated, Khaled yanked the truck's hand brake, slowing but not quite stopping the truck. It lumbered out of line. Maj. Gen. Mahmoud El-Masry, who is directing the Egyptian investigation, has been quoted as saying "Everybody thought it also developed engine trouble."

It is still unclear what happened next. One government report said a volley was fired from the truck bed, striking Sadat almost instantly. But Egyptian television, over the roar of jets, first recorded the sound of a hand grenade believed to be thrown by Khaled. Then gunfire was heard.

"I heard some explosions in front of us and suddenly I found President Sadat standing," Mubarak has said. A splinter of shrapnel sliced into the vice president's hand. The general assumption was that Sadat thought the men in the truck had stopped to greet him, something that had happened in past parades.

According to the timing of an ABC television tape of the incident, three men had leaped from the truck and thrown a grenade within the first 10 seconds. In addition to the first grenade, four others were thrown. One, a concussion grenade that only causes a stunning blast, landed behind Sadat in the reviewing stand but was a dud. Another fragmentation grenade actually hit the chief of staff who was sitting next to Sadat. But it too failed to explode. A smoke grenade did explode farther back in the reviewing stand.

Two other fragmentation grenades exploded in front of the reviewing stand's marble partition but the government said the shrapnel was deflected upward and did not cause injuries in the stand.

But the gunfire, now coming from a military assault line, was wreaking havoc. The ABC film shows that after 13 seconds, Khaled was moving steadily toward the reviewing stand with his machine gun at his shoulder with another man with a rifle standing near him. Two other men — spread out on the right and left flanks — fired supporting and covering shots.

After 18 seconds had elapsed, the film shows Sadat's photographer falling, apparently shot dead. Sadat was on the floor by then and his personal bodyguard had covered him with a chair and his own body. Another bodyguard had jumped on Mubarak.

Khaled advanced to the raised reviewing stand railing and poked his machine gun over it. He was only four feet from Sadat as he raked the area. After 23 seconds, the ABC film shows Khaled withdrawing from the stand and signaling a retreat to the other three.

At 30 seconds, the attackers come under fire. One was killed. Of the three who survived, one was shot with six bullets, another with three bullets and a third suffered only one bullet wound in the leg. Just who survived isn't known, and the Egyptian government will not say. Some western diplomats suspect Khaled was killed. (In an interview in the weekly Mayo, the official journal of the ruling National Democratic Party, Defense Minister Abdel Halim Abu Ghazala said Khaled was shot by security officers during the attack on Sadat and is lying in a coma following surgery.) Within 45 seconds, according to the ABC film, a helicopter landed at the reviewing stand. It was parked at the rear of the complex for just such an emergency. Sadat was flown to Maadi Hospital within 10 minutes. But it was too late.

According to the medical bulletin, doctors could not detect a pulse and Sadat's eyes were fixed. Blood was gushing from his mouth. He had two wounds below his left nipple, one caused by a bullet, the other by a grenade fragment. They probably caused death, doctors said. There were three other wounds in his neck, thigh and leg.

Almost every senior Egyptian government official, including Mubarak, was threatened with death from the sprayed bullets and indiscriminate hand grenade shrapnel — the strongest evidence that the plot was not part of a high-level coup. But there has been no official explanation of how Khaled's truck — one of hundreds of vehicles in a 10-mile-long parade — happened to reach the reviewing stand just as the Mirage jets distracted everyone, including the bodyguards.

Sadat's wife, Jihan, was bitter about the lapse in security. She was seen at the hospital later that day by western diplomats sobbing and repeating, "Why didn't he wear his bulletproof vest?" It seems likely, although not certain, that the plot goes beyond Khaled and three accomplices. But how far or how high may not be known for weeks. Mubarak has stressed that he will deal severely with any elements that threaten demonstrations during that period. It was Mubarak who strongly supported — some diplomats say instigated — Sadat's crackdown last month on the Moslem fundamentalists and other dissidents.

Since the investigation began there have been a number of additional arrests in Egypt but western diplomats don't know the exact number.

With the exception of the bitter but brief fighting in Assyut and smaller incidents, Egypt seems to be running smoothly. But there is no doubt that the fundamentalist movement is abroad in parts of Egyptian society. It even has become a bit trendy with the young intellectuals. A surprising number of women students at Cairo University last semester began wearing traditional veils to classes. Young men sported beards.

The veils were banned this semester after they were criticized in one of Sadat's last speeches.

It is at the government-supported university where Sadat had also encountered classroom criticism. Some educators had ridiculed his promises of prosperity for Egypt that, they argued, only affected a small fraction of the nation's 40 million. Sadat's "open-door" policy to the West following his 1972 break with the Soviet Union meant cars, cocktail lounges, television sets, and other lifestyle changes that offended Allah. In moving for a peace treaty with Israel, Sadat was doing away with old and imbedded ideas without providing a substantial substitute. Such criticism was one element of Sadat's decision last month that led to the arrest of more than 1,500 dissidents, including Khaled's brother.

But despite the arrests, Egypt is stable, and a key to Mubarak's continued stability is his close ties with the nation's military leaders. But, in turn, the stability of the generals hinges on an army of conscripts, young men who are easily influenced. Some western intelligence officials say Egyptian Army sergeants have relayed their concern about grumbling in the ranks. But the extent of this dissident movement is not really known outside of official government circles.

Mubarak, whose unopposed candidacy to succeed Sadat as president will be formally approved tomorrow, has said, "I don't think discontent exists in the armed forces." Similarly strong denials are on the lips of every Egyptian government official. A revolt within the ranks of the 367,000-man Egyptian Army, fired by a fanatical return to Moslem virtues, is the government's biggest concern. In the aftermath of Iran's fall into the hands of Ayatollah Khomeini and his mullahs, almost every intelligence agency has attempted to measure this nationalist Moslem movement in every Arab country. But western journalists have failed to measure the rumbling in the ranks of the Egyptian army.

"It's almost impossible to find out anything," said one American reporter based in Cairo, "I asked one general at a party, and he left me standing there like I had bad breath."

Observations and questions

1) These three stories present different challenges to the writer:

A) The assassination story was done after the event. The reporter is not an eyewitness. He must get near the event quickly. He must travel to a foreign country which has a different language and different attitudes toward the press. He must scramble to get every piece of information he can, television reports, newspaper stories, government releases, accounts from other reporters, and wire stories. He must sort out fact from rumor, and choose between reliable and unreliable sources.

B) Sloyan is an eyewitness to Sadat's funeral. This event is chaotic and unpredictable. Much information is obtained by eavesdropping and direct observation. The reporter must decide where to look, what to commit to memory, and what to jot down in his notes.

C) In the third story, Sloyan reconstructs the events leading up to the Sadat assassination. The reporter must investigate the conspiracy and in narrative form retell the story of the assassination, this time with more information and background. Discuss the demands on the reporter of these three different forms. What sort of versatility is necessary to carry them off with speed and efficiency?

2) Melvin Mencher divides leads into "direct" and "indirect." When a lead is indirect — that is, when it does not tell the hard news in a capsule — the writer has a responsibility to give readers reasons to continue. Such elements in an indirect lead may be referred to as "read-ons." These dramatize the news, foreshadow

events to come, create a sense of foreboding or of an anticipated surprise, or contain essential elements of narrative or dialogue. Look at all the leads in this book and identify the "read-ons."

3) Sloyan begins this story with the words "It began" — using a pronoun without an antecedent. What is the effect of this technique upon the reader?

4) Consider the structure and impact of Sloyan's sentence: "Within 23 seconds, stability in the Mideast was severely shaken."

5) In the middle of this story, Sloyan retells the events of the assassination. How does this narrative and description compare with his first-day story?

6) How does Sloyan use time as an organizing principle? How does he take advantage of the reader's general knowledge of the events of the Sadat murder?

A conversation with
Patrick Sloyan

CLARK: Let's talk about the Sadat assassination. Can you recreate for me, step by step, the reporting and writing of that story from the moment that you got word of the assassination?

SLOYAN: Well, it was an interesting day, needless to say. It started off with articles in the paper about the Westminster Government deciding to put a plaque up in Westminster Abbey memorializing Dylan Thomas. A couple of years earlier, when I was covering the White House, I was with President Carter going to Westminster Abbey and he complained that there was no plaque commemorating one of his favorite poets, Dylan Thomas. So here, years later, it turns out he has had some influence somewhere, if not in the United States. I had given him a call in Plains knowing that he gets up early, but he wasn't there so I hung up the phone, and the *Guardian* foreign editor walked over. I'm in the *Guardian* Foreign Department. For years we've given them space in our Washington Bureau and they have returned the favor over here and I have space in the *Guardian* newspaper office here in London. And the foreign editor said to me there's been a shooting involving Sadat. The initial details said that he had been wounded or hurt, and that he was all right. The first thing I did was decide instantly that I should go down there. It was too big a story to pass if he was killed. I've been through a lot of assassinations and this gives me an advantage over other reporters.

Which assassinations have you had experience with?

Hell, I was involved in the Kennedy assassination, at UPI in Washington. You know, that was an overwhelmingly big story. I covered the Warren Commission. I covered the George Wallace assassination attempt, and the attempted one on Reagan. So I know the format. I know the essence of the story, and I've written them. So that gave me an advantage.

I knew instantly from the early AP account that these were military weapons, and in that event there is always a risk that the guy was killed. Those are heavy calibre slugs as opposed to the slugs that hit Reagan. And the foreign editor recounted, after I got back, how right I was. Anyway, I decided to go, and my first call was to my wife, Phyllis. I said, "Phyllis, Sadat has been shot, or may be shot, and I've got to go to Cairo. Would you pack my bag?" An hour later she shows up with the bag, with a passport, with everything. This part is a logistics story.

What time of day was this?

This was 11 o'clock in the morning, London time. And the next thing I did was get a call back from Jimmy Carter, in the midst of all this, and he wants to know if I was calling about the Sadat thing. By that time he had heard about it. The State Department had assured him Sadat was all right. It turned out to be a bum message. It's enough when you hear a former president telling you to relax. So then I told him about Dylan Thomas.

When I got done with that I started working on the airlines and couldn't get on a solid flight out of London. So I had my travel agent work it out. I got to Paris for a 7 o'clock flight to Cairo and checked in with my office. I have a tape recorder and I wanted them to read me the latest they had. By that time they knew he was dead.

By the time you left?

While I was in Paris. The next time I talked to them, they knew he was dead and they didn't have a goddamn detail. I couldn't believe that. There was just a terse announcement. There were some other correspondents on the plane including a guy whom I knew vaguely but didn't know personally, Mike Goldsmith of the AP. He was racing in from Paris to help out the Cairo Bureau. So, I hooked up with him at the airport because he had a fixer at the airport.

Did you say "fixer?" Do you mean somebody who helps you get through customs and stuff like that?

Right. And we needed that desperately. There was a question of whether there was a coup underway. I like to do an eyeball check of the town. You've got to draw your own conclusion. The airport was the tip-off that things were pretty calm. The town was very quiet and I knew that when Nasser died the town went crazy. Eight million people in the streets.

I went over to the AP office, where they were just totally drained. It was the end of the day for them. I had hoped to be able to grab a nice long story which was going to help me do mine. Instead they had filed paragraphs here, a paragraph there, which to me was a major disappointment.

You've got to start from scratch almost.

One of the key guys there, who was really exhausted, was Steve Hindy. I revived him enough to make him go through it again. A good desk man will get more out of a reporter than the reporter knew he had. I got stuff out of Steve. Just good color, because he was there. He saw it.

So you are asking him lots of questions and taking lots of notes?

As much as I could. See, he was busy, too. I mean, he still was working so I couldn't slow him down. Whenever I saw him relaxing, I jumped on him.

Then as I'm getting in there, preparing to write, the first editions of the Egyptian papers come up and they are official government documents. In those papers were two key things that made my story so much better, I think, than my competitors'. They had the actual photographs of the assassination, the ones that many people did not see for a week or more. They also had official Egyptian statements of the events, and medical bulletins.

The Egyptian interpreter traditionally has a very slow job but people were screeching at him to read faster. Well, I benefited from one of those pictures. When you read that description of one gunman being four feet away, hosing the grandstand, that comes directly from those pictures.

Details were damn sparse then. You just didn't have that sort of stuff until those papers came up. But the Egyptian papers represent the official government view. There were just nuggets throughout those stories. I think the medical bulletin was what I was so interested in because you could tell from the description which wounds killed him.

So the chemistry of that translation, those pictures, Steve Hindy, and the look-see around town. I had covered Camp David. I had been to Cairo before, been to Jerusalem, so I knew how this would affect the Mideast peace. It's just a matter of getting control of the elements.

If I had had a little more time, I could have written it a lot better. I didn't really write that story. Maybe I wrote the top, and then the rest I just dictated. This goes back to my wire service days. Sometimes you can write even better if you speak it, and I dictated half of that story.

Where were you dictating to?

Directly to *Newsday* on Long Island. Direct telephone.

From the time you got to the AP office to the time that you called in the story, how much time did it take?

That was a little more than an hour or so, not much more than an hour.

Your first six paragraphs contain all the important elements of news and information that the reader needs in some sort of specific order, and then what follows is a kind of chronological retelling of the events in a narrative and dramatic way. Is that a structure you had in mind or did you just fall into that?

That was mere instinct. I've been doing this a long time. You know instinctively what should be up there. The goal for me in a story like that is to make it crystal clear. I don't want the reader getting bogged down. You want to make sure he understands everything you are saying. You want to be as precise as you can, then you die on every fact. Every fact could turn to shit in your hands. I mean that's what the business is about. You're not reporting people's opinions here. You're telling them what really happened. That's the crisis.

There's been a controversy in American journalism, more in television than print. It has to do with verification of information in stories like this. You were writing so quickly.

I threw out a lot of stuff that I could have put in.

Because you distrusted it?

It just didn't smell right. I'll tell you one of

them, and it haunts me to this day. The dead man — one of the attackers. The army insisted that night that somebody was killed but wouldn't identify him. A week later they were still insisting that somebody was killed. I was in Cairo a week ago and they are still saying someone was killed. What gives? I'd like to know who it was.

Several months have passed since you did this story. Looking back on it, in terms of verification, how close to the mark were you?

It holds up surprisingly well, except for the one dead guy. I would feel better if I could put my hand into his side. My first phone call was to the desk the next morning and they were very happy with the piece. I said, "Yeah, how's the stuff holding up," still in agony over the accuracy of any of it. Les Payne, the editor said, "Well, Sadat's still dead."

Let's talk about the piece on Sadat's funeral. It looks to me as if you were looking over Nixon's shoulder during the entire piece.

That's true. That makes a big difference, of course, in the reporting. You had to be there. I was in the parade. I was with Carter and Ford and Nixon, within a few feet of them almost all the way.

And you had your notebook out? You scribbled down things all the way?

Some of it. I have very good recall. I'm essentially a wire service trained reporter and you rarely hung onto anything long enough to need notes. Between the time you saw or heard something, you had unloaded it on the phone. You were done with it.

You have some beautiful description in the second piece. You have that splendid description of Prince Charles's uniform, the only person not sweating. Is that something you write down?

That was an easy recall. I mean, I can see that powder blue sash and white uniform as we speak.

Most of this is observation and, perhaps even in a sense, eavesdropping. Were you surprised when Nixon found the bullet holes?

No, I wasn't because I showed Nixon where the bullet holes were. That's known as being a participant in your own story.

And then he showed them to Carter and Ford?

In turn, right. You've got to remember here, too, that I covered Nixon, I covered Ford, I covered Carter, I know all three of them personally. It was like old home week. I saw them all before that parade. I hadn't seen Nixon since he'd been dragged off the south lawn of the White House, but he recognized me.

The story suggests a society that for obvious reasons doesn't quite have it all together. In other words, the sort of disorganization, the troops looking at each other, perhaps with some suspicion, the confusion, the bottlenecks.

Well, that's an observation you can draw. I had been to some Mideast funerals and they don't run smoothly. The band doesn't play at exactly the right moments. You are stepping into the depths of the Third World in Egypt. Seeing the Prince up close, and Carter, and Reagan or Nixon and these guys struggling to get in and the diplomat bowling them over. I turned around and I looked out at the tomb, and I saw the caisson there and the horse getting rid of these flies and I looked again, and there was Sadat's body still there. I thought, Jesus Christ, it's like an Irish wake.

Yes, everyone had forgotten about the body.

It had been totally forgotten. The whole key was to get in to see Mrs. Sadat. That was a very strong image that I wanted to make sure all my readers shared with me.

Let me ask you about Sam Brown, because he was a surprise to me. He seems out of place.

I met him in the hotel before the parade. He is a little fat, blond kid, a cute kid, dressed up with a vest on in all this heat. And I bought him some breakfast. This was early in the morning and I interviewed him. When I found out who he was, I thought that was a very interesting angle.
    Don't forget the camaraderie in here. The AP helped me the night of the assassination. Almost everything I got I gave to the AP one way or another. I know I phoned that kid into them. They'd make sure it got to where he lived. Where was he from, South Carolina? But he was part of the show, and it was an off-beat part of the show, no doubt about it. You find this Huckleberry Finn walking with all these world leaders.

In the third story you have the difficulty of retelling the assassination, this time with more information and with different details.

I take the view that you should always make another run at it, just in fairness to the reader. I mean those facts I had that first night might have been worthless, and I lacked the dimensions of the planning. I always think you should do a reprise of what has happened because as you gather more information this becomes more solid for the reader, which is the guy you've got to consider all the time. What do they know? And what are they learning?

I knew from experience that there are certain sources of unimpeachable information if you can get it, and that was the television footage. I never did see the ABC, NBC, and CBS versions. But I had a network guy who had timed them and filled me in — which goes back to the Kennedy assassination. The most telling evidence there was the Zapruder film. You took the times off that and came up with how fast Oswald had to shoot. I mean the abstraction of that kind of evidence gives strength to what you can relay to the reader.

Patrick, can I ask you some general questions about your writing habits. I am wondering whether there are things that you tell yourself consciously or subconsciously whenever you are writing a story?

It depends on the story. Some stories need very little writing skill because they are so powerful in themselves. Yet they are the trickiest to present clearly. The assassination is typical of that. That's such an overwhelming story all you have to do is present it fairly accurately.

You mean not to let the style intrude on the drama? Is that what you mean?

The facts are more dramatic than anything you can write. You can enhance the drama somewhat in presentation. But there is nothing more dramatic than just the vivid description of where his wounds were. Being as low key as you can with that kind of information is terribly dramatic. In the second story, I pretty much told the reader exactly what I saw. I remember the blood stained wall.

Do you rewrite much, Patrick? Do you have a chance to?

I write in my mind and there are some times that I will rewrite. I think rewriting usually improves things.

I'm interested in the process of writing in your mind. Can you tell me a little bit more about that? Do you mean you are playing with leads in your head as you are driving back to the office?

I'd be sitting before a video display terminal or typewriter which I use on the road. I will think the paragraph through in my mind — again this harks back to wire service training where you always sort of work in your brain. It will be pretty strong in my mind before I go ahead and write it, and once I write it, I'll look at it and see if it seems to work.

This has never occurred to me until you mentioned it, but do you think the fact that the wire service people wrote that way, that some of those leads are more readable because they were written essentially to be recited?

You've uncovered a trait of my writing now. I'll tell you, I get to where I talk to myself and I will interrupt other people around me — I mean that's how far I go.

Do you sometimes listen to it out loud, before you put it down on paper?

Well, either that or as I am doing it, and so I'm

listening to the sound of the thing as I write it, too. Sometimes I get carried away and I just start mumbling or saying it out loud.

Does that help you with things like sentence length, word order or rhythms or that sort of thing?

Oh, yeah, I really think it helps rhythm. I'm a sound person. I like the sound of words and poetry. You know spoken poetry is part of that enjoyment of the language itself. Even when you are reading silently to yourself you like to hear how they sound.

I have a catch phrase which I've used. Some people talk about reading out loud; sometimes you read "in loud." You are not making any sounds with your mouth, but the sounds are sort of roaming around in your head and you are judging the work based on those sounds.

Just like Ludwig van Beethoven. How did he get all those sounds, deaf as a post? Look at that.

Do you consider yourself old to be a reporter?

That's a state of mind and an attitude. I think this is more fun than most other jobs. It's a skill and a trade that you develop and hone over the years. You've got to be pretty good after a while, just by sheer effort or repetition. I'd like to do stories I haven't done before. I mean that was my third up front, get it all, get it together assassination. But I'd like to do stories that require me to learn something, find different formats and basically handle different information, which is the enjoyable part of this job.

Theo Lippman, Jr.
Commentary

THEO LIPPMAN, JR., 52, has written editorials for the *Baltimore Sun* since 1965 and the twice-a-week humor column "Notes & Comment" since 1976. Born in Brunswick, Georgia, and educated at Emory University, Lippman worked on a number of Georgia papers including the *Atlanta Constitution, Cordele Dispatch* and *Savannah News*. He has written political biographies of Edmund Muskie, Spiro Agnew and Edward Kennedy and edited a collection of H. L. Mencken's articles on journalism, *A Gang of Pecksniffs*. For the *Sun*, he writes editorials on the courts, civil rights, the national government, political parties, law enforcement, press freedom and related topics. During the Korean War, Lippman served in the U.S. Navy in Japan and Korea.

Rita the writer

MARCH 5, 1981

In order to save you $2.50 here's a synopsis of *Playboy's* "Rita Jenrette's Own Story in Words and Pictures":

Rita graduated from the University of Texas with honors in history and fluency in Russian. She joined the Peace Corps and was sent to Micronesia. However, she only got as far as Hawaii before deciding that she would rather sell cosmetics. The Peace Corps had no such billet, so she resigned and returned to an Austin department store.

Bored with "discussing the latest shades of nail polish," she wrote and edited a pamphlet, "The Primary System in America," which got her a job with the Republican National Committee in Washington. There she met John Jenrette, a representative from South Carolina. One night they made love on the Capitol steps during a lull in the debate on a bill. The Republican National Committee fired her because John was a Democrat.

Blonde, beautiful, fond of sexy clothes, Rita had to go out of her way to demonstrate she was a person of substance. At an embassy party, "to prove that I was no slouch, I chatted away in Russian with the Romanian ambassador," who, unfortunately, did not speak Russian.

Party, party, party. "John's drinking problem began and I came to understand the special price paid by those who live public lives." Then there was the constant handshaking at shopping centers and factory gates, the attempted seduction in the shower by a governor, that sort of thing.

Rita developed a keen understanding of politics. "When two FBI agents visited our home one Saturday morning a year ago I knew John's political career was in jeopardy." She stood by him to the bitter end — conviction of bribery and forced resignation from the House. They *almost* avoided that. John and an arms merchant asked Idi Amin to get the Ayatollah to release the hostages. Had that worked, John would have been a hero and Carter would have pardoned him. Idi said he would do it if he could get 24 of his children into U.S. schools. John tried, but the damn State Department. . . .

Rita learned John had gone to Miami to visit an old girl friend. She told a Washington reporter, Rudy Maxa, who asked where John got the money for the trip. She recalled his taking $100 bills from a shoe in his closet a few weeks before. Quick as a flash, Maxa (who may be in line for a Pulitzer for this) said, "Rita, go see if there is any more money in the closet." There was — $25,000 — and she is now seeking a divorce. John is seeking his $25,000.

"I intend now to prove myself as a recording artist," Rita concludes. If she doesn't make it there, we urge her to try journalism. Though her article is ghost written, we know she can write. There's a picture of her at her writing table, pen in hand. We've seen lots of pictures of writers. We've seen pictures of Ernest Hemingway writing. We've seen pictures of Price Day writing. Rita is better.

Observations and questions

1) William Zinsser says of humor writing: "It is a lonely and perilous calling. No other kind of writer risks his neck so visibly or so often on the high wire of public approval. It is the thinnest wire in all nonfiction, and the humorist knows he will frequently fall off. Yet he is in dead earnest, this acrobat bobbing over our heads, trying to startle us with nonsense into seeing our lives with sense." Zinsser's comments on humor come from a chapter in *On Writing Well* (New York: Harper & Row, 1976). Read the chapter and consider Theo Lippman's work in light of it.

2) Also read "Some Remarks on Humor" by E. B. White in *The Essays of E.B. White* (New York: Harper Colophon, 1977). Read some of the humorous essays of Russell Baker, Art Buchwald, S. J. Perelman, Woody Allen, H. L. Mencken, and James Thurber. Compare and contrast Lippman's work, in terms of style and subject matter, to these humorists.

3) Would you enjoy reading Lippman's columns at the bottom of the editorial page in your local newspaper? What function does humor play in a daily newspaper? Examine some papers and discuss where and how humor is used. Can humor be appropriate in news and feature stories — or does it seem more fitting on opinion pages?

4) Discuss Lippman's story ideas. Are any of his five topics surprising for a humor column? Develop a file of your own — newspaper clippings, advertisements, notes, which would lead to a humor column. Try to write a column imitat-

ing the style and length of Lippman's work.

5) E. B. White says "Humor can be dissected, as a frog can, but the thing dies in the process and the innards are discouraging to any but the pure scientific mind." At the risk of dissecting Lippman's work, consider the variety of writing techniques he uses to illustrate the lighter side of Rita Jenrette:

Hyperbole or literary exaggeration: That Washington reporter Rudy Maxa should get a Pulitzer for asking Rita if there was any more money in the closet.

Irony: "Rita developed a keen understanding of politics."

Absurd contrasts: Instead of joining the Peace Corps, Rita decided she would sell cosmetics.

Bizarre juxtapositions: The constant handshaking vs. the attempted seduction in the shower.

The false premise: "One night they made love on the Capitol steps...The Republican National Committee fired her because John was a Democrat."

Understatement and ambiguity: "Rita is better."

6) Lippman's columns have a great economy of style. Consider the mileage he gets out of a sentence fragment like "Party, party, party." Most of Lippman's sentences are short. Yet he varies the length and structure. Consider your own work in these terms.

Exercise of free speech

JUNE 21, 1981

The Supreme Court ruled 7-2 last week that a New Jersey adult book store's nude female dancers were engaged in a form of free speech protected by the First Amendment. A lot of people were surprised by this logic, but actually, it is not all that new.

Many legal experts have long said the same thing. Gypsy Rose Lee pointed out in her autobiography that, "the wimps at the American Civil Liberties Union were my best customers."

And Bubbles Gumm, in her famous course on the First Amendment at the Yale Law School, often said *"res adjudica nihili bonum!"* ("take it off").

Dorina and Her Doves made the same point in another way in the Oliver Wendell Holmes Lecture at Harvard Law. "In conclusion," she opined, "It ain't what you say, it's how you say it."

And, of course, no one in Baltimore has to be reminded of Blaze Starr's article "The Blackstonian Concept of Bumps and Grinds," in the *Maryland Law Review* (Fall, 1938).

The Supreme Court has never gone as far as it did in last week's New Jersey decision, but it has certainly been moving in that direction for years. For instance, in *Illinois vs. Paris Burlesque* 213 U.S. 105 (1959), Justice Hugo Black said for the court, "we agree this act 'doesn't play' in Peoria but, look, it's not bad, especially the LaVonne sisters."

In *Ex parte Peaches O'Hara*, 144 U.S. 62 (1968) Justice Felix Frankfurter, speaking for the majority, said of Miss O'Hara's act, "You're talking our language." The court was bitterly divided on this issue in those days. That was a 5-4 decision. In a stinging dissent, Justice John Marshall Harlan referred to Justice Frankfurter as "a weenie."

Some scholars trace the idea that nude dancing is a form of free speech all the way back to the Founding Fathers. That is wrong. It is based on a misreading of this passage from the journal of the Constitutional Convention:

James Madison. There is nothing like a dame. Nothing in this world.

Alexander Hamilton. There are no books like a dame.

Charles Cotesworth Pinckney & Gouvernor Morris. No! No!

Madison. And no one cooks like a dame.

Pinckney & Morris. No! No!

Hamilton. And nothing looks like a dame.

Pinckney & Morris and others. No! No!

Madison & Hamilton. There is nothing you can name, that is anything like a dame....

Actually, they were not talking about the First Amendment, but the Nineteenth, which they all opposed.

Observations and questions

1) Discuss the length of Lippman's pieces. Do humor columns need to be short by definition? Do you feel satisfied by the length of these, or would you prefer something longer?

2) Notice how Lippman sets up an irresistible, zany logic for his reader. Points follow each other sequentially, but not logically: "Many legal experts have long said the same thing. Gypsy Rose Lee...."

3) Lippman writes from a specific news event. Good journalistic practice suggests that even humorous pieces have some timeliness and relevance. Read your daily newspaper for any given week and identify those events that might lend themselves to this level of commentary.

4) Even the sophisticated humorist goes, at times, for the cheap laugh. Discuss the line, "In a stinging dissent, Justice John Marshall Harlan referred to Justice Frankfurter as 'a weenie.'"

5) Lippman derives much humor from contrasting levels of language. Latin and legal jargon bump and grind against funny translations and street talk. The names of legal experts are in the same soup with the names of burlesque queens. The founding fathers spout lyrics from "South Pacific." Consider how often humor depends upon a writer's playfulness with language.

6) What assumptions can a writer make about the knowledge of the audience? Do you know what the Nineteenth Amendment says? Should the writer assume that the reader can understand this from context?

White House social history

OCTOBER 5, 1981

"There has been no new china for the White House since the Truman administration. Now, breakage occurs even in the White House." — Ronald Reagan.

Notes for a social historian:

1948. After a state dinner for Winston Churchill, Bess Truman leaves White House china in kitchen sink overnight. "I'm too tired to do the dishes now," she tells Harry Truman. "I'll do them in the morning." Extreme heat, not unusual in Truman kitchen, melts platinum inlay in 54 salad dishes, ruining them.

1951. Harry Truman throws four entire place settings at television set while watching General Douglas MacArthur's farewell address to Congress. Most dishes break.

1954. Richard Nixon steals celery bowl.

1958. Dwight Eisenhower chips golf ball through window into corner cabinet. Eight dinner plates shattered.

1959. Nikita Khrushchev inadvertently shatters dinner plate to smithereens while pounding table in State Dining Room with shoe.

1960. Richard Nixon steals full place setting.

1961. Teddy Kennedy throws Arthur Schlesinger, Jr. into punch bowl, breaking bowl and several cups and saucers.

1962. During eyeball-to-eyeball confrontation on Cuban missiles, Dean Rusk blinks while pouring coffee for Russian ambassador. Hand burnt, later drops and breaks cup and saucer.

1963. John-John and Caroline get in food fight at children's table, breaking several plates.

1965. Lyndon Johnson drops beagle into

serving bowl, knocking it and several dishes to floor, where they break.

1968. Lyndon Johnson and friends toast decision not to seek reelection, then throw highball glasses and Eugene McCarthy into fireplace.

1969. Haldeman steals plate.

1970. Ehrlichman steals plate.

1971. Dean steals plate.

1972. Colson steals plate.

1973. Agnew steals napkin.

1974. Nixon steals 495 plates.

1976. Gerald Ford stumbles against waiter carrying tray of 12 dinner plates, causing them to fall and break.

1977. Rosalynn Carter destroys all highball and cocktail glasses with hatchet.

1979. Jody Powell and Hamilton Jordan get in food fight at children's table, breaking several plates.

1981. Anonymous donor sends White House $209,508 for china to replace breakage. This is free gift to nation, says Ronald Reagan, and in gratitude gives anonymous donor mineral rights to Montana.

Observations and questions

1) In the last decade we have witnessed the growth and popularity of books of lists and catalogues, serious and funny. This story is a list of sorts. Discuss the function and style of lists — and their effect on the reader.

2) How does Lippman play off contemporary caricatures of political figures to generate the comedy of this story? Is he fair?

3) Lippman carefully controls the pace of this story. The length of each passage moves the reader along at a different speed. Notice that the series of one-liners — from 1969 through 1974, using a subject, verb, object syntax — quickens the pace, rewards the reader and prepares him for the ending.

4) Notice how Lippman uses a technique which critics call "incremental repetition," or, more humbly, a running gag. Richard Nixon first appears in 1954 and reappears with greater disrepute attached to his name. Discuss the effect of this technique on the reader.

Everything you always wanted — and less

NOVEMBER 9, 1981

Director: Reagan Reelection Commercial Number One. Roll 'em.

Alexander Haig: If the Russians try anything funny in Europe, we have a plan to go to the nukes right away.

Caspar Weinberger: No, if there is war the NATO forces will only use conventional weapons.

Haig: Nuclear!

Weinberger: Conventional!

Haig: NUCLEAR!

Weinberger: CONVENTIONAL!

Ronald Reagan: Gentlemen, gentlemen....

Announcer: Everything you always wanted in a foreign policy — and less.

* * *

Director: Reagan Reelection Commercial Number Two. Roll 'em.

David Stockman: The only way we're going to get this country going again is to raise taxes.

Donald Regan: No, we've got to cut the budget some more.

Stockman: I say more taxes.

Regan: And I say less spending.

Stockman: MORE TAXES!

Regan: LESS SPENDING!

Ronald Reagan: Gentlemen, gentlemen....

Announcer: Everything you always wanted in an economic policy — and less.

* * *

Director: Reagan Reelection Commercial Number Three. Roll 'em.

James Watt: Hello, I'm the secretary of interior, but I'm not the wild man you used to see running around shouting that the federal government ought to get out of the way of western developers. I've learned to relax. That's because now that I'm in charge of conservation, I can make the government do what the developers want. Oh, sure, some people criticize me, but I DON'T CARE WHAT THE AUDUBON SOCIETY SAYS! WHO CARES WHAT THE WILDERNESS SOCIETY THINKS! WHAT GOOD ARE PARKS! WHO NEEDS THEM! THE END OF THE WORLD IS COMING SOON! GET THAT OIL OUT OF THE GROUND NOW! GET THOSE MINERALS! AND ANOTHER THING....

Announcer: Everything you always wanted in a conservation program — and less.

* * *

Director: Reagan Reelection Commercial Number Four. Roll 'em.

President Reagan: All right, all right, we will now vote for the best member of the Cabinet.

Haig: Haig!

Weinberger: Weinberger!

Stockman: Stockman!

Regan: Regan!

Ronald Reagan: And I vote for my buddy here, Boog Powell.

"Powell": Sir, I'm HUD Secretary Samuel Pierce.

Announcer: Everything you always wanted in a Cabinet — and less.

Observations and questions

1) Expert writers understand that punctuation and the mechanics of print can be liberating devices. Consider how Lippman employs these to recreate patterns of speech and help organize his story: capitalization, exclamation points, ellipses and the stars that divide the sections.

2) Lippman writes a parody of Lite Beer commercials, which are themselves humorous. Try to imitate this technique by placing a political character or public figure in the fictional scenario of a familiar commercial.

God on trial

DECEMBER 10, 1981

Judge: Call the next witness.
Bailiff: God!
ACLU Attorney: I object! God is not on trial here.
Arkansas Attorney General: He's an expert witness.
Bailiff: Do You swear to tell the truth, the whole truth and nothing but the truth, so help you You?
God: Of course.
A.G.: Where were You in the beginning?
God: I was hovering over the void.
A.G.: And what did You do?
God: I separated light from darkness, created the firmament, earth, vegetation, the heavenly bodies, birds, fish, beast and man.
A.G.: The latter in Your own image?
God: Yep.
A.G.: No further questions.
Judge: Cross-examination?
ACLU: Yes, your honor. You are the Supreme Being? The Creator? the First Cause?
God: Numero Uno, that's Me.
ACLU: So who created the void, which preceded You?
God: You don't create voids. Voids are, like, nothing. Formless. Chaos.
ACLU: But You said You were hovering over the void. How do You hover over nothing?
God: You're just playing with words. It's a question of semantics. Let's define our terms.
Judge: Get on with it.
ACLU: Okay, when You were listing Your accomplishments You were reading from something. What was it?
God: Genesis. I needed to jog My memory.

It was a long time ago.

ACLU: Who wrote Genesis?

God: I dictated it to Moses.

ACLU: Did he get it exactly right?

God: Oh, close enough. This was before shorthand, you know.

ACLU: It says here creation took six days. It says You created sea creatures and birds one day, beasts and man the next. Is that correct? Man after the lower animals?

God: Oh, yes. That I remember very well.

ACLU: Was a day 24 hours, as it is now, or could it have been, say, a million years or more?

A.G.: I object!

Judge: Overruled.

God: I guess it could have been a million years. I'm not even sure I said "day," now that you mention it. That may have been Moses's word.

ACLU: Is it possible that what Genesis really says is that man evolved —

A.G.: Objection! Objection!

Judge: Overruled.

ACLU: — from the lower creatures after a day of millions of years?

God: Well, again, it's a question of semantics. I guess you might put it that way.

ACLU: No further questions.

Judge: Redirect?

A.G.: Are You now or have You ever been a secular humanist?...

Observations and questions

1) With a group of friends read this aloud as if it were a play. Does this piece work as well when read aloud, or is the dialogue clearly designed to be read silently? What is the difference? Consider the difference between dialogue in a play and dialogue in a novel.

2) Lippman's dialogue contains clear echoes of the famous Scopes Monkey Trial of 1925, a trial which pitted Clarence Darrow against William Jennings Bryan. A newspaper account of this confrontation is reprinted in *A Treasury of Great Reporting*, edited by Louis L. Snyder and Richard B. Morris (New York: Simon and Schuster, 1962). Read this account and discuss Lippman's work in light of it.

3) What dangers are there for the writer in putting words in the mouth of God, especially in a comic context? Is there a chance he will turn off readers otherwise inclined to be persuaded by his arguments?

A conversation with
Theo Lippman, Jr.

CLARK: Maybe we could start by talking about ideas. Where do you derive your ideas for columns? What sort of things are floating in your mind now?

LIPPMAN: I don't write 100 percent broad lampoon or satire. Sometimes I write things that are somewhat serious but are really off the main road of editorial pages. Perhaps you saw Mary McGrory's column saying that though she's Irish, she grew up on Winnie the Pooh, and she's for the British going to war against Argentina.

I was thinking of trying to write a piece about how much the English language really does unite these two countries and affects their politics and national relations. In fact, a lot of us side with the British on political questions because of the literature we were raised on. This is not an original thought but it's something that I haven't seen anybody talk about lately and I thought I would like to do it. I've been very depressed about the sort of war hysteria that's been built up over the Falkland Islands. It's such a complex, moral issue.

Another idea: I notice that two of the books that won the Pulitzer are about the Civil War. I'm sort of a history buff. I might write about how the Civil War has continued to fascinate scholars and the public all of these years.

What would be the tone of that one?

It would be sort of light. Even when I'm serious I try to avoid sounding serious. Probably my staple is to use anniversaries of Americans, generally not quite first rank, like President Tyler.

Say today is President Tyler's birthday and then give a thumbnail sketch of him, maybe tongue-in-cheek but always factual. Saying he married a redhead and declared war on Mexico the next day, or something like that.

But then I try to make a point about our history and our contemporary politicians. They are really human beings, and we are human beings who write about them. We shouldn't get so serious that we divorce ideas and issues from the common humanity that we — the writers and readers and politicians — share. It is easier to do that, I've found, about somebody who has been dead a long time than it is about somebody who is a senator or president or governor today. I enjoy doing those as much, or perhaps more than I enjoy doing the straight, broad, burlesque-type funny pieces.

Are you combing the news to find stories?

Yes, I'm sure that 80 or 90 percent of the pieces I do are suggested by a story that was in the paper within a week of the time that I'm writing. For example, one of the columns makes fun of the seeming divisions on every major issue among the Reagan senior officials. There had been a number of stories emphasizing one or another of these disputes. And not long after — I think my piece came out first — there began to be more analysis pieces bringing it all together. I think the column makes an honest point, and it's funny at the same time.

Do you have a file of story ideas? Do you clip out pieces?

I clip out stuff and pin it on a bulletin board here. I don't have a filing cabinet. And I keep a sheet of paper on which I write down ideas because I have a terrible memory. If I just say, hey, this would be a good idea, then when I get to work the next day, I forget. So I have to clip or write myself notes. I read a lot of papers. That's my research system. I also read different calendars, you know Chases' calendar which has everybody who was born, or every important event that took place on each day. I have several of those.

You say you have a bulletin board? Are you looking at it now? I mean is it over your desk?

It's across from my desk.

What things are tacked up there?

Well, the first thing I see is an ad of F. Lee Bailey for Smirnoff which came out on the back of *Newsweek* the day that the story broke about his arrest in San Francisco.

For DWI, right?

Yes, that's right. Then, next to that is something called "300 Ways To Use This Newspaper" which I clipped out of the Waco newspaper where my daughter works. And none of those 300 ways has anything to do with editorials or editorial pages or columns or anything.
    But as for other story ideas, there's one here on exile. I write our editorials about legal issues and law enforcement, and prisons, and so forth. I was reading a review of a new book about prison reform which makes a point that about 200 years ago many western countries dealt with prisoners by just ordering them to leave.

Send them to Georgia.

Yes, that's right, and this was particularly effective in this country. Since they stopped doing that, we had to start building a lot of prisons. And I was going to write a "Notes and Comment" saying that instead of parole, Maryland should send people to Georgia.

As a matter of fact, I have a special problem in writing "Notes and Comment." Many times, the humor of it will depend on saying something that is absolutely not true, putting untrue words in people's mouths, words that they never uttered or creating situations that never happened.

The constitutional definition of malice is to say something that the writer knows is not true. That's part of the definition. We had a court case here a couple of years ago, which was recently upheld, in which the disc jockey said something that he knew was not true. The state judge said that alone made it constitutional malice. So one of the notes I have on the bulletin board is to try to find some way to write about that in "Notes and Comment."

In other words, if you have Gypsy Rose Lee making a point of law or something like that?

That's right. Under Maryland law now, if Alexander Haig said that I never made this statement and I say I knew that when I wrote it....

And so did everybody else who read it.

Yes. Well, the court said that if any rational, or any intelligent reader could have assumed that he in fact said it from reading this — then it's malice and libelous. By the way, every word in the Rita piece is true. Slightly recast, but in fact, you know, she does say for example that she studied Russian and chatted away in Russian with someone who didn't speak Russian, and that sort of thing. A couple of more clippings I've got. I've got a clipping from the *Wall Street Journal* that says *Rolling Stone* is asking people to subscribe to it for the local library. Others, you know, are putting pressure on the city or county to stop subscribing. A clipping from the head of our library here talks about how expensive books have gotten. I was thinking of combining the two and suggesting also that our library start buying second-hand books which are cheaper.

I'd do it in a sort of funny way. We have a little running feud going between our city library, which is trying to be an old-fashioned library getting serious books that will keep for ages, and our county library, which is one of the most innovative and successful in the country. It goes strictly for best-sellers, then turns around and sells them off for 75¢ a year later. So I thought I could be both humorous and still make a serious suggestion. That's some of the things I've got clipped up.

Most Pulitzer winners and most of the ASNE winners are works of significant length and dimension. Yet the judges were impressed by the brevity and the economy of your work. Are most of your columns about this length?

We have a space designated for "Notes and Comment," and it takes about 375 to 400 words, and we have arbitrarily decided never to exceed that. I think once in six years I have written the piece longer than that. I think it's great for two reasons. One is it forces you to rewrite. So there's never any padding. If you just have to rewrite and then rewrite again and again, you are going to turn out the best piece you are capable of doing. I think if I had to write 800 or 1000 words I would not say any more and I would not say it as well.

The second thing is that I feel a short piece can be read in a hurry. It doesn't cause anybody to stop and say wait a minute, to reread it. If it's clear when it's that short, even if it's not funny or not rewarding in any other way, people forgive you. I mean they will only spend a couple of minutes, and I don't think reading a bad piece will turn them off to your byline.

What role are you playing as a humorist in the paper? You hear all sorts of comments about the general depressing nature of news.

This column can do three things. It can humanize politics. It can humanize the editorial page. I mean it can remind people that we are individuals with quirks and so forth. And it can tranquilize the day's headlines. As bad as the news is, there are still some other things. This is life and we can live with it.

I don't think that every editorial should have that tone. We wouldn't be doing our job if we didn't get angry and denounce people that we think are doing wrongful things. But you need a little change of pace on the editorial page. This is one way to do it.

Do you see yourself as a part of any tradition of writing, people like Baker, Buchwald, Mencken or Swift?

It would be presumptuous of me to name some names and say that I am in their tradition. But let me tell you the people that I have read who have influenced me. One is Will Rogers. One thing I have not mentioned earlier about this column is that I try to keep anger out of it. I think Rogers was good at taking the events and personalities of politics of his day and maybe ridiculing and criticizing them and putting them down but never with much acid. Price Day, who was editor-in-chief here and who originated this column, is another.

I didn't know who he was. You mentioned him in the Rita column.

He was editor-in-chief here for many years. He created this column. It might be silly one day, and it might be very serious the next, and yet somehow, over the years, he made it possible for people to accept the column that did a variety of things, which is a very hard thing to do. It has made it easier for me that people have come to associate "Notes and Comment" with a form of writing that has great latitude.

I think I've tried to write the sort of satire that Richard Armour does. A fellow named Will Cuppy wrote several books back in the 30s, 40s, 50s that were histories of the world told in humorous fashion. He was rewriting history books the way I rewrote Rita Jenrette's article with absurd juxtapositions and strange cause and effect.

How do you know something you have written is funny? What sort of tests do you have? Do you have occasions in which you think something is particularly juicy and then falls flat?

If I think it's funny I go with it. I think my judgment is pretty good, but sometimes it isn't. In fact, the most recent piece I did (about the Falkland Islands) probably fell absolutely flat.

Haig went to London the first time and he said, "I don't have any American solutions in my kit bag." I thought that was awfully funny that he would use that phrase. I haven't heard it in years, and it seemed to fit. The whole idea of this war was so Victorian and everything. So I wrote a piece in which a custom's agent goes through Haig's kit bag as he arrives in London and takes out all these things that are his troubles, and I thought it was very funny.

Yet everybody that I asked said it just didn't come off. In the first place, a lot of people, I was surprised to find out, had no recollection of the words of the song, so some of the puns were just misleading.

The pieces that I'm not sure about, I don't show to anybody. The pieces that I think are really funny, I'll show to an editor here who is particularly good. If on a scale of 1 to 10 I think something is an 8, I go to him, and maybe we can get it up to a 9 or a 10. But if I do something that I think is a 2 or 3 I just slip it in the paper and say well, I guess the people will forgive me this time.

Is each piece individual in terms of its tone or do you have some general categories of humor and satire that you rely upon?

I think that this business of dialogue or even monologue is a good way to get a lot in a short piece. I use that quite a bit. The Rita piece is where I parody/summarize an article or a book or perhaps a long speech. I use that a fair amount.

You take something presented in a straightforward way, even if it's in *Playboy*, and retell it with your own point of view.

That's right. I look for a target that is easy to ridicule, and recast it. I think when I am really trying to be funny and nothing else, I will use one of those devices. For example, one I'm fiddling around with right now is Reagan going on radio to bolster his popularity. I was thinking it would be good to do a piece on him as a call-in host and nobody calls in, to show his lowering popularity. Again that would be just a monologue with him talking, talking, talking, talking, talking.

Are there taboo subjects for humor? I'm thinking about something that happened here at a seminar for editorial writers. A discussion leader had everybody try to write a humorous piece on the spot, and he suggested two or three topics, one of which

was "Whatever Happened To the Libyan Hit Squad?" About 10 people tried their hand at that and did some interesting work. But there were two journalists from Texas who could not bring themselves to write about an assassination squad. Because of the Kennedy assassination in Dallas, they couldn't see any humor in it, and they couldn't understand how anyone could apply humor to it. So we got into an interesting conversation about that. I am wondering what your perception is on that? Would you write about the Libyan Hit Squad? Did you?

I didn't.

Are there subjects that are taboo?

Sure there are. If you write a column like this, you really depend on the respect of people who read it. If you write something that offends them, maybe one piece wouldn't do it, but if you write two or three over the course of a year I think you would lose that part of the audience. So you have to be very careful about what you write. But, having said that, I think there are very few things that the humorist can't touch. I think you could write about the Libyan Hit Squad.

How about abortion?

Somebody was saying the other day that if you can get the Right To Lifers to understand that nuclear war will kill fetuses they will join the Peace Movement. I don't think that would offend even a Right To Lifer, and so I think you can employ humor in almost any area.

Was anyone offended by your piece on Creationism?

The "God on Trial" cross examination is a much abbreviated and slightly recast recapitulation of the real Scopes trial. It is arrogance and being a bully for somebody who thinks of himself as intelligent to be picking on the Creationists. In the first version I wrote, that was clearly the case. And I said I think a lot of people, not only Creationists but those who are quite religious, are going to dislike this piece. And a lot of people who are really on my side will say what's the point. I mean if they're that wrong, and if it's that obvious, what's the point of somebody in a big powerful newspaper even jumping on them? It's just not fair.

I just didn't like the piece, so I went back and read the Scopes coverage. The *Evening Sun* had run seven or eight columns a day, and they had practically a verbatim account of Darrow's cross examination of Bryan. Darrow wasn't really ridiculing him. He was saying that maybe this is just a difference of opinion about the way to explain things, and I hope my piece reflected that. I was having as much fun with the ACLU as I was with the state of Arkansas.

I see you using both understatement and hyperbole or exaggeration. Are those tools in your tool box?

Yes. I think there are a limited number of tools and anybody who wants to write is going to fall back on them. I used to use cliches in editorials and in other writing, thinking that well, this phrase became a cliche because it quickly conveys precise information to a lot of people and we ought to use cliches because people read newspapers in a hurry and so forth. But I started using cliches in the mouths of people in "Notes and Comment" to suggest that they are unoriginal people. Then I came to think that maybe that's everybody's reaction to a cliche, so I've stopped using cliches in my editorials.

Maybe we can conclude by talking a little bit about your writing habits. Do you write on the typewriter or VDT?

I write on the VDT, and for somebody writing a short piece, it's far superior to a typewriter or long hand or anything else. You can edit, change one word to another and still have a clean copy in front of you. And on a short piece like mine you can scroll it up and down in a matter of split seconds. So you don't have the problem of rewriting that you have with something a couple of thousand words long.

Do you do any written preparation in advance of the first draft? Are you inclined to make an outline at all?

I may make an outline on a legal pad, in a sort of 1, 2, 3, 4, 5, 6, 7, 8, 9, 10 points that I want to make. Then maybe I'll look at that and decide what sequence I want to put them in. And I take a few notes as I read.

Let me ask you this, because it's something that I'm fascinated with, and that's how the process of writing is also a discovery process, a learning process, if you will. In the Rita piece, for example, when did you discover the line "Rita is better?"

It should have been "Rita looks better." I've been sorry that I didn't make that clearer. When I started that piece, it was about her as a writer, and that became then a series of jokes and innuendos of a sexual nature. You know, *Playboy* pictures and that sort of thing. I just didn't want to do that. I don't remember if I had that line to begin with but I had the idea in mind that I wanted to say something about her and Hemingway and Price Day. I just kept trying to do it a different way and finally struck on the summary, and just pushed that down as what seemed to me a logical conclusion.

Another example. How about the idea for putting "There is nothing like a dame" in the mouths of the Founding Fathers. Do you remember when that struck you?

No. I set out to do the whole thing on excerpts from precedents, because the point I wanted to make was, these two things didn't go together, the First Amendment and nude dancing. I think I got all the humor there was out of the idea that these precedents had gone too far. It occurred to me that obviously that's not what the Founding Fathers had in mind and "There is nothing like a dame" just came along.

By the way, I hate to keep criticizing myself. I thought after I saw that in print that instead of saying they were not talking about the First Amendment but the Nineteenth, which they opposed, I should have said the Nineteenth, on women's suffrage. A lot of people who read that wouldn't know for sure what was going on.

How do you feel about Art Buchwald winning the Pulitzer?

It is gratifying to know that the people who have the most to say about what is recognized in journalism are more concerned about humor as a serious component of the editorial page than they have been. Jack Rosenthal of the *New York Times* won the Pulitzer for editorial writing, and apparently had a humorous piece in there. We hear at the National Conference of Editorial Writers conventions every year that we've got to get more humor on the page. A lot of papers are looking for ways to do it. The *Evening Sun* here, our sister paper, has a feature of little one-sentence gags. The *News American,* the other afternoon paper, has just started something of that sort. A lot of papers will have institutional, unsigned editorials that are clearly funny. That's very difficult to do. If you go to something and your mind is set to receive serious matter, you miss it. That's what's so nice about "Notes and Comment." The tradition and format are such that people are alert that it's not meant to be taken all that seriously.

Tom Archdeacon
Sports Writing

TOM ARCHDEACON, 31, now writes sports for the *Miami News*, but before beginning his newspaper career he worked as a bartender, greens keeper, and high school English teacher. He applied for newspaper jobs throughout Florida without success until a small paper near Miami hired him as a sports writer. "I had never written sports," says Archdeacon, "so they hired me." He later became a stringer for the *Miami News* and has worked full time for the *News* during the past six years, the first three years on the high school sports beat. Born in Ottoville, Ohio, he graduated from the University of Dayton with a degree in English.

More than just a race queen

FEBRUARY 12, 1981

DAYTONA BEACH — Rudy, the grimy mechanic with L-O-V-E tatooed across the knuckles of his right hand, stood gap jawed and staring. When he finally got his breath back, all he could manage to babble was something about having sweet dreams all night long.

It had all taken him by surprise. He had been helping Tom Sneva, the Indy racer, and his pit crew with their Buick in the Daytona Speedway garage yesterday afternoon. They had been working since early morning, not even bothering to break for lunch. They had too much to do. The important 125-mile qualifying race would start in less than 24 hours, the Daytona 500 was just four days away. The car wasn't running its best and this was Sneva's first race at Daytona.

Across the way, Linda Vaughn was making her rounds. White mohair cowboy hat, long feathery blonde hair, satin blouse, tight, tight jeans, white cowboy boots, long red fingernails, fluttering eyelashes, diamond rings, gold chains, gold hearts...all decoration on one of the greatest figures anyone could ever fantasize.

She was like a magnet the way she drew men to her.

Rudy saw her first. She walked straight toward the Sneva car and soon the whole crew was tripping over wrenches and cords, trying to get close to her, only to stand in awe, bashful, punching each other in the ribs, giggling like schoolboys. They would hurriedly wipe away the grease so they could shake her hand or, better yet, pray for a kiss on the cheek. A mechanic ran to the truck for his Instamatic, "I want a picture for my mantle," he gushed.

Linda Vaughn is the Babe Ruth of beauty around the race track. She's been around the stock-car scene for 20 years, a 38 Double-D oasis in a sea of noise, grease and sheetmetal. Once Miss Atlanta Raceway and Miss Firebird, she's now the Miss Hurst Golden Shifter and one of the company's public-relations agents.

A few years back Stock Car Racing Magazine ran a special section on women in racing. In it she was described as "the most popular female in racing history." Nothing has changed.

Matched against her curves, Daytona's high banks seem like a path for kiddie cars. As she walked around the garage yesterday, talking up her sponsor, meeting old friends, captivating new ones, she made dream circuits overheat.

"I love racing," she said. "It's in my blood, has been since I was little. Racing attracts good, wholesome people. I'm glad they accept me as their racing lady. They're all like family, from the drivers I grew up with, Richard Petty and Cale Yarborough, to the grimiest little mechanic. I'm married to racing."

* * *

But the romance has been anything but roses. Later, away from the fawning crowds, she sat in the STP office and talked about the other side of the sport, when the tires quit squealing and the engines shut down. It's the story of a wholesome Georgia girl coming of age in the midst of stock-car men, probably the most ardent group of male chauvinists in all of sport.

As Vaughn talked, the lines near her eyes peeked through the makeup. In her late 30s, she is still beautiful and still very busy. Although she was tired and had a trade show to do that night, she wanted to talk. She had something to say.

"You know," she said, nodding toward the garage area, "today was the first time in 20 years I was allowed in that garage area officially. I mean, I'm trying to establish different patterns now. I'm not just a race queen anymore, I'm a business person, a sponsor. Some people in NASCAR looked at me as nothing but blonde hair, a big chest and no brains. Finally, they are thinking like they are in the 20th Century. They have a new executive vice president, John Ritter, and he's responsible for some of the new ideas. But there's been times in the past, even though I've devoted my whole life to racing, that I've been treated poorly."

Up until a few years ago many tracks did not allow women in the pits or garage areas. There were even signs posted, "No Women." To be a race queen was about the only way a woman could be involved in big-time stockcar racing. Janet Guthrie got a few Grand National rides, but now she's back home in New York, out of the sport because she can't find sponsorship. There are still no women mechanics or crew chiefs. Basically, the rule is no women, except race queens.

The reasons for this stance have never been made clear, although privately some drivers and NASCAR officials will still rattle off a litany of excuses. Things began to change a bit in 1973 when a woman photographer threatened to file suit. Vaughn got into the sport through the beauty-queen door, now she's trying to pry the other doors open.

"I'm trying to help push for a lot of improvements," she said. "I had a compound engineer from one of the tire companies come up and tell me she was afraid she wouldn't be able to do her job at Daytona, because of some people's attitude. I wrote NASCAR about our problems. I'm pushing for a nice area to be put in for the drivers' wives. I think I can do some good. I'm used to fighting battles."

Although she doesn't belabor the point, she admits there were problems early on with the women, as well as the men.

"Some of the wives used to sit outside the fence and be drinking," she said. "They'd see me go in there with the men in my sexy little costume and they really got on me, made it real tough. They didn't know I meant business with all this. Finally, it took my momma and Fireball Roberts to straighten them out.

"And there's a NASCAR guy that ridiculed me. He didn't understand this was my job. I'd come on Sundays wearing a sexy little skirt with a slit up the side and he'd make comments. I told him, 'All those fans don't come to see your legs, buster.' I help sell our product, I help put people in the stands. People didn't know where I was coming from."

* * *

She came from Dalton, Ga. and has loved racing since she was a kid.

"I remember my first race," she said. "I slipped off one Saturday night, went down to the race track and climbed up a tree to watch. I had that red Georgia clay all over my legs when I came home. My momma gave me a whipping and the next week I did the same thing.

"Finally, my momma realized I liked it. We had a small dirt track there and I really grew up, so to speak, that summer. They decided I should be the girl to give out the race trophies."

She was still in high school when she entered the Miss Atlanta Raceway contest. "There were four judges, three men and a woman," she said. "I stared that woman right in the eye and finally I could tell she approved. And it didn't hurt me, putting my long hair in one of those french twists and just filling out my bathing suit better than the rest of the girls."

She became Miss Firebird the next year. She'd ride the Firebird float at each race, smiling, waving, throwing out her chest and telling everyone how she just loved the sport. As soon as the good ole boys could recover, they'd want to rush out and fill their tanks with Firebird gas.

She's been the Hurst Golden Girl for 14 years now, promoting at races, trade and auto shows, doing commercials and a couple of movies.

"All the magazines have approached me, especially *Playboy*," she said. "They offered me a lot of money, then went to one of my driver friends and offered him a lot if he'd pose with me. I don't think we need to promote our sport like that, plus I'm not interested in taking my clothes off, except with someone I care about. Anyways, I promised momma I wouldn't. Now I'm not saying I wouldn't do some sexy pictures. I think the race fans are entitled to that.

"But I think being top-heavy has hindered me. It's kept me out of being a commentator, kept me out of doing a lot of TV. They think I'm too sexy. I realize sex got me here, but I think it's the gray matter upstairs that will keep me here. It's like Dolly Parton says, 'I don't sing with my chest.' Well, it's the same with me. I want to be known for everything I've got to offer, not just a big chest."

She checked her watch. It was getting late and she still had a trade show to do. She got up from the STP office and headed for her car, stopping to chat with a mechanic who wandered past carrying a gas can. As she left, she pulled him close and pecked him on the cheek. Then she rushed off.

She might not want to be remembered for her looks, but they are hard to get off your mind. Like the mechanic, he had walked off in a daze, leaving the gas can forgotten in the grass.

Observations and questions

1) Archdeacon carefully describes Linda Vaughn. Along with the details of her clothes, make-up and jewelry, he refers to her as "a 38 Double-D oasis in a sea of noise, grease and sheetmetal." (A mixed metaphor? Should an *oasis* be in a *sea*?) He says, "Matched against her curves, Daytona's high banks seem like a path for kiddie cars." Look carefully at the details of Archdeacon's description, along with the connotations of his words. Is this simple leering, or does Archdeacon use the description for some higher purpose?

2) In each story, Archdeacon delays the introduction of the main character. He prefers to open with a scene or an anecdote. Is there too much delay here? Doesn't Archdeacon run the risk of losing his reader before the reader gets a chance to meet Linda Vaughn? Or are the first paragraphs interesting and provocative enough to encourage a reader to read on? Apply this test to all of Archdeacon's leads.

3) The writer breaks the story into three parts. What purpose does such a division serve? What are the major themes and concerns of each section? What picture emerges of Linda Vaughn's character?

4) Notice how Archdeacon provides a sense of closure with an ending that echoes the beginning. Many good stories conclude with this feeling of the circle being closed. Search for other examples of this technique and experiment with it in your own stories.

The ringmaster of Miami boxing

MAY 18, 1981

The spotlights beamed down, the crowd waited. All eyes were on the ring where the muscular young boxer shuffled nervously in his corner. The other corner was empty.

The wait became longer, more uncomfortable. Bad timing for such a lull. It was the first bout of the evening and the crowd was in no mood for a big delay. A few people began to shout. The promoter began to panic. The excitement was dying, turning to unrest.

The corner remained deserted.

The missing boxer, a Pahokee truck driver new to the fight game, had started into the arena when his trainer suddenly realized the guy had forgotten the protective, plastic cup in his athletic supporter. The trainer quickly pulled the nervous kid back into the dressing room for the alterations.

Suddenly a familar voice boomed from the public-address system, defusing the tension, reassuring the fans. It was Frank Freeman, the dapper, 70-year-old ring announcer, who once again began to weave his magic. The corners of his deep-set blue eyes crinkled into crow's feet while the mischief bubbled out with the sparkle.

"OK folks, I want to let you know that the other boxer will be out shortly," he said. "He has left off some of his equipment, something which is essential to him...but wasted on me."

The crowd snickered.

"He'll be out here as soon as they find one large enough to accommodate him," Freeman said wryly. The crowd roared. And when the edgy boxer finally did appear, there were no boos, just one thunderous round of applause.

This was Frank Freeman at the Sheraton Beach Hotel fights. It was Freeman at his best, working the fight crowd the way he used to work the high rollers at Kitty Davis's Airliner on the Beach, and the classy crowd at Carnegie Hall, even the two-bit gawkers who gathered in front of his sideshow tent back in his circus days. They were the ones he lured with stories of Woofoo the Fire Eater and Ajax the Sword Swallower.

For the past 23 years Freeman has been the voice of Miami Beach boxing and wrestling. Besides the hundreds of undercard fights, he figures he has worked nearly 40 world-title bouts. Once the spotlights are on, Freeman becomes showman, ringmaster, defender of good taste and at times a bit of the Artful Dodger.

Several years ago, when a wrestling fan threw a coin into the ring that struck him below the eye, Freeman grabbed the microphone and challenged the offender. "Chances are you got an edge on me, but come on up here and we'll settle it," blasted Freeman. "And nobody will argue about the decision, we'll fight to the finish."

Then there was the time 4,000 fight fans crammed Miami Marine Stadium to watch the closed-circuit boxing show of Bob Foster and Muhammad Ali fighting the Quarry brothers. Suddenly the picture fizzled out. Promoter Chris Dundee had already gone, leaving Freeman to deal with hundreds of angry fans. Police feared a riot.

Finally Freeman let each person come on stage to air his gripes. When anyone asked for a refund, Freeman said it was impossible, that the money had been loaded onto a speedboat and taken to a vault on Miami Beach. The ploy worked.

"Frank is a master," said Dundee. "He has been a lifesaver for me. Many times when people were unhappy, he's stood up and made them smile. Whenever we had big shows and I was nervous as a leaf, he was a daddy to me. He calmed me down. He is a beautiful man."

The seeds for that showmanship were sowed a long time ago, back when Freeman was still a brash teenager growing up on the streets of New York City. He left home to work circus sideshows, then became a pitchman for various medicine shows and finally emerged as Freeman the Hypnotist, the Man with the Radar Eyes.

"I've always enjoyed the limelight," Freeman admits. "I think I wear it well."

* * *

The old picture is comical, and yet a bit haunting. It shows a somber man, his hair slicked straight back, a pair of round, old-fashioned pince-nez clipped to his nose, a tiny waxed handlebar mustache above his lips, a Van Dyke goatee jutting off his chin.

It is a photo of J. Francis Freeman, the 47-year-old lecturer, graduate of many colleges, world traveler, expert on hygiene, mental health and human sexuality.

It is a souvenir from Freeman's past, a time when he was a superb con man who could weave his spell on a paying audience and then slip out the back door, at times, one step ahead of the cops.

In truth, this goateed authority was nothing but a 21-year-old kid. Frank Freeman in costume. The glasses, the black bow tie, the waxed mustache were all props. He toured the country as one of the nation's foremost experts on health and yet had no college degree, not even a high school diploma. He had left the classroom at 16, finishing his education on the streets, hustling pool games, chasing girls and occasionally rolling a drunk.

The son of a Hungarian fur nailer, he sought excitement not only in the city's nightlife, but also the boxing ring. But the two didn't mix and his vigorous training did nothing but wear him down. A doctor suggested a sabbatical in the country. Freeman worked a month on a Long Island truck farm before the carnival lights lured him from the potato patch.

"The farmer took us to the Riverside County Fair, and I ended up in front of the Dreamland Circus Sideshow," he explained. "I was fascinated by the sideshow talker. I went in the back and asked the boss for a job. He gave me a chance, so I went out, made the spiel and turned a tip. When I finished, people came in to see the show."

The following year he got a fulltime job with the show, which by then had hooked up with the St. Leon Brothers Australian Circus. The next season he returned to New York City and acted as a pitchman for various stores. He hawked everything from rubber exercisers and eucalyptus leaves to psyllium seeds.

"The seeds gave you added life. They removed poisons from your system, purified your blood, regulated your bowels," Freeman boasted.

Where did they come from? What did they contain?

"I'll be a sonofagun if I know," Freeman said, smiling.

A few years later he joined a vaudeville troupe, teaming with Raffles, the magician whose speciality was escaping from a steel memorial vault. Then he toured on his own, as the phony health lecturer. Before he decided on the professorial look, he wore a doctor's white coat and hung a stethescope from his pocket. He claimed to be a moonlighting Bellevue Hospital physician.

"All the time I was polishing my suggestive abilities, never realizing they'd materialize into hypnotism," said Freeman. "Then one day we played a date and a theater manager asked us if we had any other act. I told him we'd give him a hypnotist. I'd been reading up on it and the next thing I knew I was walking on stage hypnotizing people. I became quite good, called myself Freeman the Hypnotist. Radar was big then, so I became The Man With the Radar Eyes. That was 40 years ago and I still perform some."

Frank Freeman has always been the same. He never let a situation intimidate him. That's how he peddled his herbs, that's how he courted Anne Rothenberg, who became his wife.

"Her family didn't go for it at all," said Freeman. "Anne was going out with a lawyer and here I came along, a phony hypnotist, a ham actor, a knock-around guy who didn't have a dime."

Anne laughed at the memories.

"He was quite a man, like a god to me," she said. "I left the poor guy I was going with standing outside until he nearly died from pneumonia. Three days after I met Frank, I proposed to him. Ten days later we were married."

* * *

The boxing and wrestling rings are Freeman's only stages these days, except when he dusts off the hypnotic act for a special occasion. He is working on a book manuscript about his days as the roguish health professor and says he may revive a sleep-inducing record he made in the early '60s. He figures it might sell on late night TV.

But those ventures are simply sideshows. Freeman has been a bonafide businessman for a quarter of a century, selling industrial real estate in Hialeah. Some years back he was named the president of the Miami Springs-Hialeah Board of Realtors.

So are there really two Frank Freemans?

"Not really," said Freeman. "In the last 40 years, I have conducted myself in an honorable manner. I've treated people with respect. I discovered many years ago an expression they use in the carnival — 'the wise guy sleeps in the Hoosiers' barn.' I learned the thief, the hustler, the wiseguy is eating chickens one day, feathers the next. It finally got to me, that's no way to live. The square sleeps in a clean bed, has three good meals. By being diligent and honest, you can go farther. I've changed...."

Then he paused for a second, as if tempered by some inner voice. Slowly the mischief bubbled up from his eyes and a tiny chuckle trickled off his lips.

"...Not that I don't use a little joke, a little con now and then...."

And then he walked off with a fight fan, a plump woman who nearly overflowed her white stretch pants.

"Say, you're losing weight aren't you," Freeman said with sincerity. And the lady suddenly smiled, swept up in his magic. The phony glasses were gone, the hair had turned gray, but the huckster's heart was still sound.

Observations and questions

1) This story begins with a humorous anecdote and depends more on anecdote than other Archdeacon stories. Discuss the effect of the opening anecdote on the reader. Does Archdeacon tell the story too quickly? Not quickly enough? How do you decide how much detail to put in an anecdote, especially at the top of the story? Examine the rest of the anecdotes in the piece, discuss their placement and impact. What techniques lead to the recognition and collection of useful anecdotes?

2) Many anonymous characters populate newspaper stories. Consider the love-struck mechanic at the end of the Linda Vaughn story and the plump woman in the white stretch pants at the end of the Frank Freeman story. Each character performs important work in the story. Discuss the following questions about the use of anonymous characters:

    A) Does it hurt the credibility of the writer to use anonymous characters?

    B) Is it fair to a grimy mechanic and a fat lady to use them, presumably without their knowledge, to improve a story?

    C) Is it possible that the mechanic or the lady would recognize himself or herself in Archdeacon's story? Does that matter?

    D) What sort of reporting and observing skills are necessary to find these characters?

Carl Joseph's celebration of the human spirit

AUGUST 27, 1981

DAYTONA BEACH — Bobby Frazier walked to the center of the football field wearing a pith helmet, monogrammed sunglasses, maroon and gold shorts and shirt and long white socks. He carried a clipboard in his hand, a pack of Red Man chewing tobacco in his hip pocket, a whistle perched between his lips. With one shrill blast his practice was over.

The Bethune-Cookman players ended their drills and jogged over to their coach, surrounded him, then dropped to their knees for one last sermon. From this sea of helmets and bowed heads, a pair of wooden crutches stood upright.

They were Carl Joseph's crutches.

They rose above this group, just as Carl himself had done in the afternoon workouts. For whenever Carl Joseph is concerned, there is more than just an exercise in football skill involved — there's the celebration of human spirit.

Frazier talked to his troops about striving for greatness. As he did, he glanced at those crutches and the athlete that leaned on them. Frazier is big on teaching through example. He himself was a successful mix of athlete and academician. He was a record-setting Bethune quarterback in the early '60s, then a professional baseball player and now holds a doctorate in education. But Frazier knows there is nothing as convincing as Carl Joseph, his freshman linebacker.

Joseph plays football on one leg. He was born 20 years ago without a left leg, a handicap he has refused to yield to no matter what the circumstance. He was a versatile athlete for Madison (Fla.) High, starting three years of football as a noseguard, playing basketball well enough to dunk, high jumping 5-foot-10. He ended his remarkable high school career with 13 athletic letters.

And that is where most people figured it all would end, preserved in the memory book with the dried up prom flowers and the old graduation pictures.

Joseph's triumphs have not gone unnoticed. He has had dozens of testimonials in the football world, been on television, had a book written about him and soon will have a movie.

The Television Corporation of America will start shooting a made-for-TV movie in a few months. Joseph will play many of the scenes himself. He signed a contract in June with TCA for approximately $400,000. An advisory group of Madison citizens, headed by restaurant owner Jimmy Wyche, is helping him handle his finances, investing the money until Joseph will be assured an income for the rest of his life.

With his newfound prosperity, Joseph plans to move his mother from their weather-beaten little house in Madison's run-down black "Quarter," as it is known. And he has thought about getting himself a customized van.

But even before the riches came, most people figured the story would have to end with high school. The next step would have to be college football — and with one leg that would be too great a leap for even someone like Joseph.

Then he double-teamed the doubters, using sheer gumption with a simple defiance of logic and human limitations. It didn't hurt that he banged a few heads in his first day of college practice, then ran a grueling mile and a quarter on one leg before backing it all up with a battery of windsprints. By the time he was finished, he had cemented himself into the Bethune-Cookman football scene.

He is not on athletic scholarship. Friends and admirers are paying his college fees. Donations have come from as varied a group as a Miami Beach lawyer and a Daytona Beach sporting goods store owner to the St. Louis Cardinals football organization.

Although he is not being carried financially by the Bethune athletic department, he'll probably bring the school as much or more publicity than some of its greatest athletes — Larry Little, Bobbie Clark, and Cy McClairen included.

"People don't believe a lot of the stuff they hear about me," said Joseph. "So I got a lot of them always watching me, a lot of pressure to perform everytime I run out.

"Before it was all for them. I wanted to prove I was like the others, that I could play football. I did that. Now I'm doing it for myself. The fellows are a lot bigger and faster here, but I think I can make it with them. I want to prove a guy with one leg can play college football. Nobody has done that before. It might sound unbelievable, but I had to deal with that before."

* * *

It was time for the linebackers' agility workout. Joseph's crutches dropped behind him into the grass and he hopped onto the practice field on his muscular right leg. The coach sent the players shuffling backward, forward, to the left and the right, all with just a quick point of the finger. There was sudden change of direction in starting and stopping and Joseph was handling himself beautifully, mixing strength and incredible balance.

Then, suddenly, he slipped and fell over with a hard thud.

"Get up Carl!" yelled the coach. And quickly Joseph was back up, lunging forward on his massive leg. It is so developed that although he said he is just 30 inches around, he buys his pants with a 36-inch waist so he can slip them over his muscular right thigh.

Next came a drill with a defensive player against two offensive players, a blocking back and a ball carrier. Carl took his turns, sometimes getting knocked down and once in a while shunting the blocker and grabbing the ball carrier.

He proved his salt nearly a week ago during one of his first Bethune workouts. Lorenzo Wilson, a 210-pound junior fullback, had been the blocker on the drill.

"I didn't know if he could really play in this league," said Wilson. "I was supposed to be the lead blocker and I thought I'd take him light. But Carl hit me so hard, he knocked me back into the ball carrier and we both went down. I was shocked, devastated. I had a headache the rest of practice, but I knew the guy was for real."

Rod Carter, a speedy running back who was All-State at Daytona Mainland High, knows too.

"I ran the ball on a touch-off drill and all of a sudden he was there and tackled me," said Carter. "He stuck me hard. He had moved laterally for 10 to 15 yards all to the opposite side of his leg."

Joseph underscored those plays with a little locker-room advice. "That they just overlooked me was their first mistake," said Joseph. "I told them to be alert because when I come, I come wide out. Especially now. I'm an underclassman and I've got to prove to these guys that I'm one of them."

That's nothing new. His junior high school coaches would not let him play football because they thought he couldn't handle himself. And after high school he said his coach told him to forget any thoughts of college football. Even Frazier didn't want him at first.

"I was afraid to even let him come out," said Frazier, "especially if he ever got in when we were winning a game. I thought if I put him in, someone might take their frustrations out on him.

"I told him we couldn't make the drills special for him and he told me point blank he was a football player. The first few days I kept a close eye on him so he wouldn't get in a drill and get hurt. The more I watched, the more I realized he could take care of himself. He's strong up top and has amazing balance. I've never seen such a quick recovery time. He gets knocked down and hops right back up.

"He'll play some for us but I think his main area will be blocking as an up-back on our extra-point and field-goal attempts. He's quick and can hold that block long enough."

Joseph's main contribution, Rod Carter thinks, is in the example he sets. "If you can do that on one leg, just think what we should be able to do on two," said Carter.

That is never more evident than on the windsprints that end practice. If someone slows down, Joseph will charge straight over them as he comes barreling along on his crutches, like a skier wound up to 78 rpm. He makes one run after another, arms straining, leg churning, face grimacing.

And when practice finally ended the other day, Joseph trudged over to the water spigots with his teammates. He dropped his crutches back into the grass and stared at them for a second. "I bet they're glad for a rest themselves," he said. "I give 'em a workout. I punish 'em."

* * *

Lunch was over and Carl sat on a bench beneath the trees in front of his dormitory. He wore some old cut-off football pants from his Madison High days and a new goatee he was trying to grow. He graduated in 1980 and sat out of school for a year. By this summer he had ballooned up to 235 pounds. Now he is back down to 195. Two-a-day practices in the sun have trimmed him down as much as anything.

He looked at the practice field. Soon he'd be out there running again. He smiled. Now the place was deserted except for a few practice dummies strewn about, the blocking sled and the homemade goalpost at the south end of the field.

Actually, the field at Bethune is a rather enchanting place. As the daily drills go on, old-timers, a few college students and some girlfriends gather under the shade trees at the edge of the field and watch Frazier and his players.

Bethune football has a personal touch and Joseph wants to be a part of it. Down the line there was talk of a scholarship to the University of Pittsburgh once he brought his grades up a bit. But the deal was to be a manager or a trainer, not a football player, so Joseph turned it down.

"I talked one-on-one with Jackie Sherrill and he could tell I didn't want to be a trainer," said Joseph. "I didn't want to stand on the sidelines, I wanted to play.

"I'd like to be a high school football coach. That's why I'm still playing. I want to get more experience. You can't just read it out of a book. I think I should be a good example for kids. Football is just like a game of life and I know how to play that."

Then he looked at his watch and hopped up. "I'd better get some rest before the afternoon practice," he said. "It's already 1:30."

Actually, it was 1:15, but Joseph sets his watch 15 minutes ahead these days.

"I do it to make curfew," he said. And then he walked away. He never wants to be late. He is not a man of excuses.

Observations and questions

1) The writer calls Carl Joseph's athletic skills a "celebration of the human spirit." Yet some groups of disabled citizens resent newspaper and television stories that fall into what they call "the super cripple" category. Dozens of films and television shows celebrate the courage of those who have overcome crippling handicaps. Discuss the moral value of such stories, reader fascination with them, and Archdeacon's treatment of Carl Joseph.

2) Archdeacon gives us a fascinating detail about the massive development of Carl Joseph's leg: "It is so developed that although he said he is just 30 inches around, he buys his pants with a 36-inch waist so he can slip them over his muscular right thigh." Does that detail whet your appetite for more? What is the circumference of Carl Joseph's thigh? How does this compare with the average male of his size? Has he ever been given a Cybex test, which measures leg strength? What is his jump reach? Can you think of any other relevant measurements? Do you think such a discussion would be appropriate and informative?

3) Sometimes Archdeacon receives criticism for writing long stories. For the sake of argument, imagine that you are Archdeacon and have to cut 20 percent out of each story. How could you make it shorter without ruining the story? One good rule of thumb: Brevity comes from selection and not compression.

The pride of Bucktown

DECEMBER 24, 1981

Boarded up and broken down, they all stand empty...the old church, the grocery store, the ladies' wear shop, the rooming houses, the pool hall. Silent tombs covered with scrawled graffiti and pools of broken glass.

This is NW 3rd Avenue, through the heart of Bucktown, a place where the paint is faded and the heydays forgotten.

As the cold evening began to settle in last Saturday, life went on as usual. Down at the corner where 11th Street cuts through, an old man in a maroon jacket and shades stood in front of the record store and the bail bondsman's office, sipping malt liquor from a brown paper bag as he sang the blues. Two dozen long-robed women and men in denim jackets, disciples of a black religious sect, marched past quickly, their chants drowning out the old man's song.

Two men walked by carrying half of an overstuffed living room chair between them. They tugged it down a side street and threw it on top of a bonfire that had been built on the curb in front of a rundown tenement. Sparks sprayed up, dancing above the heads of the men who drank and laughed in the firelight.

It was just another day in the Bucktown neighborhood of Overtown...and then again, it was very different. It was down in front of Fat Sam's Bucktown Pool Hall where the young men began to gather. The air of excitement and anticipation that came with them mixed with the clatter of pool balls and the jukebox music that rose from inside.

Some of them wore fine felt cowboy hats, others the black and white Bucktown ball caps. Their duffel bags were filled with football gear and neighborhood pride.

These were the unbeaten Bucktown Bucks, the best semi-pro team in the Miami Football League. In a couple hours they would play the Liberty City Hawks for the league championship at Miami-Dade North. They met at the pool hall which, along with Bessie's restaurant down the street, is where the players gather before games.

At that very moment, just 18 blocks away, the Miami Dolphins were battling the Buffalo Bills for the championship of the American Football Conference's Eastern Division. But the world of pro football and the game played in the ghetto are worlds apart.

"For us, Bucktown winning is just as important as when the Dolphins win, probably even more so today," said Charles (Bunky) Clark, the colorful team owner, starting fullback, street hustler and pied piper of Bucktown. "Most people in the community here can't afford $10 for a ticket to the Dolphins. Even if they did come up with $10, they'd keep it and find out the Dolphin score on TV.

"Bucktown football is guys you see every day. It's street versus street, seeing who's the best, but usin' the football field instead of battlin' and fightin'. It means something to the people here and usually it's free."

As he talked, Bunky stood on the corner, several dollar bills wedged in his fist. He spoke to a little man in a black hat and a heavy overcoat topped with a fluffy fur collar. The man carried a small brown paper bag to hold his money. Although a ten-spot might not be that easy to come by for the average local folks, the hustlers and street-wise gamblers seem to be able to come up with a decent bankroll.

"The line on the street for this game is six points," Bunky said. "We've beaten them three times, but they've gotten pretty good here at the end of the season. I got $1,500 bet on this one myself. There must be $10,000 or $12,000 bet on this game. I saw two dudes put down $4,000 each."

It was action like that, Bunky said, that helped Bucktown get its nickname.

"There was always someone hustling and gambling and selling something down here," Bunky explained. "Hustlers would come around from all over and there was money circulating and things would be happening. Some of the boys a few streets over in Swamp City said it reminded them of a movie picture Fred Williamson was in. It was a story about a little Southern town where things were wide open and pretty corrupt. The movie was called *Bucktown*. The Swamp City boys said that's just how it was down here. The name stuck and got stronger as it went along."

Each Overtown neighborhood had its own idiosyncrasies, its own characters, and consequently, its own bragging rights. The sporting field became nearly as important as the street corner. In the early days there were the Eighth Street Bulldogs and the 20th Street Sharks and a kiddie football club called the Baby Browns. The Bucktown Bucks got their start about seven years ago.

"It started out with the dudes from the pool hall on Third Avenue playing the guys from the pool hall on Second Avenue," Bunky explained. "Then we said let's get some uniforms. Some guys ended up with shoulder pads, some didn't. Then Swamp City started playing and the Mean Machine and a couple other teams and after a few years we had ourselves the start of a league."

Ron Taylor, a tight end for the Bucks, remembers those early efforts.

"It used to be short pants, a couple of pads and they'd knock the blood out of ya'," said Taylor. "This has come a long way. In the old days some guys played barefoot, some had sneakers, but there was no cleats. When big John McGriff from the U-M played here, he just wore a helmet and shoes, no pads or uniform. This year everything was regulation."

Except for two years ago when the Bucks went 6-4 and got into the title game, Bucktown hasn't had much to brag about. "Last year," said Taylor, "Bucktown was something like the New Orleans Saints of a year ago. I think the team's record was 1-10."

This year things changed. The Miami Cougars of the Florida Football League folded before the season began and several of the players joined the Bucks. Then Bobby Felts was brought in as the new head coach. A Northwestern High graduate, he had played at Florida A&M and later had brief stints with the Detroit Lions, Baltimore Colts and Montreal Alouettes.

The team went 11-0-1 during the regular season, including six shutouts. Carol City's 13 points were the most anyone scored against Bucktown and only the 22nd Street Outcasts could manage a tie, that a mid-season 6-6 deadlock.

"The Bucktown team had been strugglin' so long, but it never won," said Livingston (Zam) Joseph, a former Miami Cougar linebacker who had come from the Virgin Islands. "The cats would play, but they never had a coaching staff, never had to compete with each other for jobs. It was favoritism ball, but a lot of other people didn't want to come down to Bucktown and play. The area had a bad name."

Quarterback Ritchie McFarley agreed with Joseph. A Miami-Dade Community College graduate, he lives in Allapattah and had played for the Cougars, too.

"There used to be a lot of us afraid to go to Bucktown," said McFarley. "They had a lot of rough people hanging out over there. But a lot of the Bucktown folks wanted something good to happen. People adjusted and did the right things. They saw how hard we were working to make the team something to be proud of. And the Bucks do mean something to the community. We're a good football team, but we're also showing something positive is happening in Bucktown."

* * *

The chartered bus pulled up to the corner of 11th Street and Third Avenue and parked alongside the old Economy Drugstore.

The drugstore, like the grocery and pool hall next to it, is abandoned. But the pharmacy's old advertisement is still whitewashed on the wall — *"We fill ANY prescription."*

It was below this sign that a dozen Bucktown fans lined up to give the team its sendoff. The players — fellows who've given themselves names like Nugget and Ironhead and Nap and Bull and Donald Boy — filed past. When lineman John Linnear trudged by with a leather jacket and a cowboy hat that had a great plume of feathers trailing off the back brim, one of the bystanders cracked..."It's the ghetto cowboys."

But beneath the fancy trimmings is a blue-collar team with some big-time dreams. "Most of the guys here are workin' men," said receiver Eddie Hudson. "Cooks, security men, garbage men, construction workers, a mechanic, a truck driver. We come here for recognition. A lot of us couldn't afford to go to college or didn't have the grades or came back home. We get our recognition with the Bucks."

Taylor, the 30-year-old tight end, sat halfway back in the bus and quietly talked about what brought him to this team. Linnear sat directly in front of him and listened. George Cox, a linebacker, with star earrings, tinted glasses and a bandaged right foot, sat alone with his crutches. "Stopped a bullet with my foot up on NW 74th Street," he said, shaking his head. "Some foolish, jealous fellow up there just shot me."

Bunky sat in the front of the bus, a roll of bills still snug in his fist. A few seats away sat running back J.C. Crump, the only Bucktowner ever to make it to the big time. He played seven seasons in the Canadian Football League. Now he had returned home, back to where it had all begun.

Such was the case with Taylor, too.

"I graduated from Northwestern High in 1970," he said. "I was sort of small back then and never played any football. I played the trumpet and the bass horn in the band and got a music scholarship to Florida A&M. But I left there after a summer and came back to Miami-Dade. That's when I got started with football. I live on NW 34th Street now, but I grew up in Overtown. Probably half the team has roots that tie them back to Bucktown."

As the bus pulled into the Dade-North parking lot, a hush fell over the team. Linnear leaned back and whispered, "I told you, Ronnie, high school was a long time ago." They both smiled and left the bus.

Inside the locker room the players taped and padded themselves for the game. They had new uniforms, the same silver and black as the Oakland Raiders. A few dressed themselves further, wearing their personalized hand towels like loincloths that bore such fearsome warnings as "The Assassin" and "Dr. Death." And there was the defensive back who had decorated his helmet with decals, the way college teams do when their players make big plays. But his paste-on awards were simply orange smile buttons he had gotten free with his junk mail.

Although a lot of the players thought Bunky had bought the uniforms himself, he claimed they came from the community. "Since we had been so bad before, we kept braggin' this year," Bunky explained. "We pushed ourselves. Different stores finally said if we went to the playoffs they'd buy us uniforms. They never figured we would, but we held them to the promise. They cost $2,500."

Crump sat in the middle of the room and watched the scene. "There are a couple guys in this room that could play professional football," he said. "And there are guys here that just want to get a chance at college ball."

He is the exception. He is also the hero. After graduating from Miami High he played parts of two seasons of junior college football before moving to Canada as the youngest player in the CFL's history. He had left Miami a college dropout and returned a pro football player with a five-figure contract and a new cream-colored Cadillac, complete with a brass running back on the hood.

"But I was released last August by the Ottawa Roughriders," he explained. "I was picked up by Toronto, but refused a three-year contract with them. I came back here and started up with Bucktown. I was drafted by the Buffalo Bills in 1977 and I'm going back there for a tryout in the spring.

"In the meantime I'm a part of the Bucks again. Last spring we held a three-day mini-camp and recruited all around the city. We wanted to build a foundation for things to come and it looks like we really have."

The players gathered around Felts for The Lord's Prayer and then the low guttural chant began, "Buck...Town...Buck...Town...Buck...Town."

"A lot of us dream of making it to a pro camp," said McFarley, the quarterback. "We all hope someday we'll meet someone with connections. There's been a couple people at our games we didn't know. They said they were scouts. We didn't have any way to check them, so all we can do is just go out and play...and hope."

* * *

During the week before the game, Liberty City's big defensive end, Gary (Too Tall) Hill, had appeared on a local black radio station boasting about what was going to happen to the Bucks. The comments had angered some Bucktown players, but they figured it was just hot air. After all, they had beaten Liberty City, 7-0, 13-0 and 19-0, during the year.

But with temperatures in the low 40s and the small crowd (unlike the nearly 2,000 that attended several of the home games at Gibson Park) huddled quietly in the stands, Too Tall's words were a steamy threat on this cold night.

Bucktown fumbled the ball away on its first two possessions. The second turnover turned into Liberty City's first score. The Hawks had stalled, but Bucktown cornerback Bernard Wright roughed their punter to keep the drive alive. A play later, Liberty City quarterback Bill Ferrell completed a 29-yard touchdown pass over Wilson to receiver Eddie Daniels. For the first time in four games, Liberty City had scored on the Bucks.

Hawk defensive back Sylvester Wooten decided to rub salt into the wounds. He pranced to the Bucktown sideline and began ridiculing Wright, "Hey No. 6, where are ya'? Don't be hidin'."

On Bucktown's next possession, McFarley was chased into the end zone for a safety and Liberty City had an 8-0 lead. And on the next possession the snap went over the punter's head and out of the end zone for still another safety. Liberty City led, 10-0.

Bobby Felts, his mood about the same shade as the old, red Alouettes' overcoat he wore, called his team together on the sidelines. "I'm tellin ya' good buddies," he said, spitting the words through the tiny gap in his front teeth, "forget those pretty new uniforms. You don't look pretty. You're blowing everything we worked for all year."

Felts is known as a fellow who doesn't mince words. He took over the team in the beginning of the year with a no-nonsense attitude and soon some players, including several big linemen, quit.

"We figured he'd change," said McFarley, who is Felts' stepbrother. "But he told us he'd rather walk down a dark alley with a few good men that would stay and fight, than with a bunch that would turn and run. He didn't change, he just worked us harder."

"Harder than Dick Vermeil works the Philadelphia Eagles," Bunky had said earlier. This time Felts' speech seemed to hit home. And from the stands came the chant of an old man, the same old man who'd stood on the street corner that afternoon and sung the blues ..."Buck...Town...Buck...Town."

If it was Felts scolding that began the thaw, it was that old man's lone cry through the cold that seemed to warm the Bucks up. In the first possession of the second quarter, McFarley threw a 19-yard touchdown pass to Bruce Crump. Too Tall was hurt and left the game limping. Wright, the much-maligned cornerback, picked off two Liberty City passes.

Liberty City defenders started to go after McFarley, hitting him late and roughing him whenever the chance arose. But with just a minute left in the half McFarley scored on an eight-yard run. Carlos Meza added the extra point and Bucktown had the lead, 13-10.

In the locker room at halftime McFarley sat slumped on a table, an ice pack pressed over a lump on his cheek. "Their game plan was passed on to me earlier this week," McFarley said softly. "They planned to get me out of the game."

Before the third quarter began, a spectator with a diamond chip on his ear worked his way onto the Bucktown sidelines. He goaded Bunky the first chance he got. "The spread is six, sucker, you're gonna lose $500."

Liberty City fumbled on its first possession and with one long pass Bucktown was down to the Hawks' three-yard line. Bunky took the next handoff and burst three yards for the score, giving Bucktown a 20-10 lead. He immediately trotted out of the end zone, bee-lining straight back to the sidelines where his tormentor still stood. "Now, you owe me the $500," he growled through his helmet.

Liberty City never scored again. Bucktown won and took home a golden, four-foot trophy. It was getting close to midnight when Felts slipped out of the dressing room. He had to go to his night job working school security downtown.

And the team headed back to Bucktown for the victory celebration. "We've got champagne iced down, a bottle for every player," said Bunky. "And there's Bull and fried chicken and pigeon peas and rice. It's time to party." With that, he folded his new bankroll into his pocket, smiled and said, "It's been a decent night."

* * *

By the middle of this week the last of the champagne bubbles had evaporated, leaving only the delights that an unbeaten season can bring. Fat Sam wore his Playboy T-shirt and a toothless grin as he talked to the fellows that had gathered on the bench in front of the pool hall.

J.C. Crump sat watching the familiar street scene that swirled in front of him. A teenage boy in an old, black sport coat and broken-down sneakers peddled joints around the corner. Two young kids kicked a can back and forth across the sidewalk. A young girl carried her baby on her hip.

"I'm tied to Bucktown," Crump said. "I was born and raised here. I'm never gonna forget, this is what got me where I am today. The football I know, I learned off these streets.

"The place has been put down because of the crime down here. But the way things are going, people are gonna start coming back. We've gotten rid of some of the bad guys. We're trying to build something here. People here look up to this football team. We want to start little league football. We can give the kids a different model. We want them to go back to school. If sports gets them there, fine. Even if I should make it with Buffalo next year I'm not gonna forget this place. I'd like to build me a Boys Club in Overtown. We need to change things for the better."

As he talked, two little boys pressed their faces against the front window of the pool room. They were staring at the gleaming trophy the Bucks had won Saturday night. It stood on Fat Sam's desk beneath the "No Pot Smoking" sign.

Bunky sat on the wooden bench next to the racks of pool cues. Peaches and Herb sang from a suitcase-sized radio as four teenagers shot eight ball.

"I grew up right here, where the houses used to be at Dixie Park," said Bunky. "Then my momma moved to 10th Street. I had a real strong street reputation back then. The older dudes would give me a buck every time I scored a touchdown on the little kids' team. But I was persuaded by the guys I ran with that bein' on the street was the thing. The place where it was really happening. So I went to Booker T., then to Jackson, then to Northwestern. Never did play football in high school though, I liked the streets too much.

"Then I learned it wasn't all that's happenin'. So now we're trying to change attitudes, trying to convince the kids to stay in school. We've had some kids make it from here too, guys like Vernon Delancy and Tony Rogers. They're both on basketball scholarships at Florida. Even the little dudes that I have walk my dog — I'll give 'em five bucks, if they keep their grades going. But the way they listen is if they respect you, if they envy something you're doing. That's why it meant so much for the Bucks to be so good this year."

From the radio came The Ohio Players singing about the holidays. The music stirred Bunky's own Christmas thoughts. He looked around the room and pointed to Fat Sam's desk. "My Christmas present is that trophy over there," he said. "We created the league and now we finally won it. That is the best gift we could have."

Ron Taylor went one better. "This championship wasn't just the best thing to happen to Bucktown this Christmas, it was the best thing to happen in years...hell, make that a decade."

Observations and questions

1) Archdeacon is known for his unconventional approach to sportswriting and his off-beat story selection. "The Pride of Bucktown" is a good example. On a day when the Miami Dolphins had an important football game, Archdeacon writes about minor league football in the black community. What role does such a piece play on a sports page? Is Archdeacon's off-beat approach a service or disservice to the reader? To what extent should a journalist reflect the attitudes and interests of his community? To what extent should he help to broaden the interests of his readers?

2) The game narrative is central to this story, yet Archdeacon draws a broader picture as well, one of a town and its people. How does the writer use the game narrative to reflect the values of the players? How is this game narrative different in tone and style from those you might read of a professional or major college game? Archdeacon says "the world of pro football and the game played in the ghetto are worlds apart." Cite instances in which the writer elaborates on this theme.

3) Sports excite and fascinate people because they reflect in miniature the values and concerns of the culture. Honor, pride, courage, teamwork, perseverance and revival are celebrated in the rituals of the game. How does this play out in Bucktown?

A conversation with
Tom Archdeacon

CLARK: Do you get many assignments, or do you choose your own stories?

ARCHDEACON: I select my own stories. I get an assignment once or twice a week, maybe to do something with the Miami Dolphins, but the rest of the time I get to do what I want and in some ways that's good. In some ways it's not because you can only grow so much. You need somebody to pump ideas in there.

I think a typical reaction to these stories might be, well, these are awfully offbeat, unconventional sports stories. I wonder if you could talk about that. Is that characteristic of your work and what's behind that?

To be truthful I get bored with the mainstream of sports. I'm not interested in statistics and, to tell you the truth, right now I can't tell you who's leading the American League and National League. I don't really care.

But I'm fascinated by some of these little backwaters. A lot of people think I'm stretching a point here, but I'm just fascinated by these people and I think their stories are a lot more interesting. They inform a little bit, in their own way, and they also entertain. I think there is room for them in the paper. These people really pour their souls out to you. When I get around the Miami Dolphins it's just not the same. At least half the time, I've got what they'll say down to a formula, and I don't really like it.

Where do you find your ideas?

I've got a network of people who call me. They know I do these kinds of things, and I just hang around the seedy bars looking for them. I watch when I drive through town. I live in Homestead so I've got about a 30 mile drive, and I take different routes. I'm always looking for something a little different, and a lot of people know that I like to do these things, so they call me. Once you get one person, it kind of spreads. I go through the *Miami Herald* and our paper and others. A lot of times I find stories that I've really got to stretch my imagination to get them in the sports page.

Can you give me an example? What are you working on lately?

I'm doing a story on Kid Gavilan and a fellow named Bobby Dykes. They fought 30 years ago in Miami for the welterweight championship of the world and it was the first time a black man and white man had fought in Miami. Kid Gavilan won. I guess it's the classic story. Today Kid Gavilan is down in a seedy hotel in Miami and has nothing. Bobby Dykes, the fellow who lost, owns a string of bars here, has an insurance company and is pretty well-to-do. I spent two or three days with Kid Gavilan in this hotel and walking around town with him, because he has no car. Then I went down with Dykes and got a membership in his club and hung out there for a day or so to get the feel of it.

Next week I go to Key West. On the way down I'm stopping to do a crabber who catches blue crabs down on Florida Bay and he's got some wild tales. He's being run out because people are coming in, like all the refugees, and stealing his traps. He's the last of the crackers down here. Then I'm going down to Key West. There's a fisherman down there named Cap'n Tony. I'm going down and talk to him for a little bit, and then I'll see what else I can find while I'm down there.

You seem to find more food for your imagination in the NASCAR circuit and in box-

ing, not in the mainstream sports. Is that a correct observation?

That's true. Boxing's probably one of my favorite sports. My girl friend says how can you stand two fellows beating the hell out of each other? The boxers will really pour their souls out to you, and you see everything stripped away. They'll cry. Everything just pours out of them after a match. And before a match you can just see it build up and there's nothing, no other teammates there, no p.r. men, nothing like that. And with the NASCAR circuit they seem to be very approachable people. A lot of them have colorful tales, and it just fascinates me.

I also see you doing a lot of stories out of the black community.

In fact, that helped get me fired from one paper. Not too many black people got the paper and one of the fellows who ran it, one of the higher-ups, pulled me in one day. He talked to me and showed me the circulation figures for all the parts of town where the black people lived. He said, "How many people buy the paper there?" Of course, there were not many. And he said a lot of the other people don't care to read about niggers, got it? And I said, yeah, I got it. I went out and wrote three stories about black people three straight days, and blew their pictures up real big on the page, and got fired.

Weren't you teaching English to black students at one time?

Mostly black students, basic English, 18-year-old kids who were ready to graduate and couldn't read. But the school system had a policy that said let's move them out of here. They're 18 and they've got children and everything else, let's get them the hell out of here. But they weren't prepared for anything. In the grocery store, if it didn't have a picture of a tomato on the can they didn't know it was tomatoes. And so instead of an English class it turned into just getting them ready for making it on their own.

So your contact with that community has been extended into your sports writing?

Right. When I taught school, I coached a Little League team in the black community and did a lot of little things. After that people started to feel that I was sincere and I cared a little bit. So now a lot of black people call me up with a story.

Were you called upon to work in Liberty City during the riots?

I thought I could go down and get a story from some of the people during the riots, so I talked to the managing editor and she said well, if you want to go down, go on down. I had done some stories down there when I had the high school beat, but I didn't really have a contact.

I called this community center. I said look, here's who I am and I'd like to talk to some of these people, and just ask them why they're doing this. He said well if you want to come on down, there are some down on the street. So I got a photographer friend of mine and a black reporter went with us. They rode in the front and I rode in the back.

When we pulled up down there, a crowd saw the white driver and started trying to get around the car. I got out of the car and he left. It was 200 yards to the community center. I couldn't get there. I got surrounded by a crowd. People started pushing and shoving and then somebody grabbed my shirt and it ripped. They were spitting on me and everything. One guy stepped forward. I was trying to tell him what I wanted to do, but I was shaking. I couldn't get it out. And this one guy kinda stepped forward and shielded me a little bit and said let the cracker talk.

And so I said, hey look, you tell me whatever your beefs are, because all you're doing is burning up each other's properties. The people in Coral Gables are just shutting their doors and looking at the smoke through the window. They don't care. The one thing you don't have is communication with them. This way, whatever you tell me, I'll put it in the paper. This is your chance to put your message in there.

This guy calmed them down a little bit so I went to this community center and five or six guys came in and started talking. One guy said, look I want you to come with me. He took me down to his apartment in some old flop house and showed me where the rats had eaten through and his baby had been bitten by a rat. The sinks didn't work and garbage was in the stairways. He was telling me about the landlord who comes over and picks up the rent. He's hired this big gorilla to come and if people don't pay up he throws their stuff in the hallway and puts a padlock on the door. So I got the story. That's the same area I went down to for the story on Bucktown later.

Tell me about that story.

When the championships came they called me up and asked if I cared to do a story. So I went down, and one person was my guide at first. He got me down there and let everybody relax a little bit. Then I came down a couple of days to the pool hall and a couple of other places they hang out. Then I rode with them on the bus to the game and hung out with them there. They had a party afterwards. I stopped by the party and the next day went down to the pool hall and spent some time. I got a little feel of what had just happened.

Why weren't you down at the Dolphins' game doing a sidebar?

Some of my fellow sports writers wondered the same thing. Even some of the people in Bucktown were a little surprised. I just said I think it's a lot better story. Some people scoffed at it at first. In fact, one said, "You might be getting into a Bucktown rut." I said well, what is another sidebar to a Dolphin game? We've had 15 years of Dolphin stories. We've had so many sidebars I just thought this would be something a little different. I think they thought I was trying to get the day off or something at first, and you know it turned into a lot more work. I went down there at noon and left at three in the morning, but it worked out fine.

Tell me about Linda Vaughan. At the beginning you reflect her traditional cheesecake role, but it seems that once you got a chance to talk to her alone, a whole different picture of her evolves.

I read a piece on her once and I had seen her — you can't miss her at the races. I started wondering who in hell would want to be a race queen for 20 years. Auto racing is a pretty chauvinistic sport. They don't even like women in the pits.

She had this little trailer down there where she gave out this p.r. stuff so I just followed her when she came to the track. Oh, I was just 60 feet behind her and she didn't even know I was there. I watched her go through the pits and watched how everybody acted and watched her go through her spiel.

After 45 minutes I came up to her and introduced myself and told her what I wanted to do. I said look, I'd like to talk to you a little bit and I just wonder how you can do this for 20 years? It struck a little cord in her. We talked, and she seemed appreciative that somebody didn't just want to talk about her chest or something like that. When we finished I made like I was going to leave, but I just kind of stayed there and watched her go back out and on came the sex queen thing.

Do you have any special interviewing techniques?

I've got pretty long hair and I scare some people. I walk up to them and, especially the older, more conservative ones say, "What the hell is this? It can't be a sports writer. It's got to be some guy who's riding a motorcycle or something." But once they see this guy is not going to grab their wallet or say something crude to them, I don't know if they're relieved but they almost talk more to you. I think if you really try to put yourself in their shoes and not take the highbrow approach they open their hearts to you.

Sometimes people I deal with aren't too familiar with sports writers. They've never been interviewed and probably never will be again. Sometimes they tell you things they shouldn't. If it's just something that you know bares their soul, well fine. But if it's going to embarrass them ...when I get done with my story I just run through it once with my name in there, asking myself how I'd feel.

In the Frank Freeman piece, you talked to his wife. Do you like to talk to relatives?

Don McNeal is a player for the Dolphins. He was number one draft choice for the Dolphins one year. There was just a little blurb in the *Miami Herald,* and it said "Don McNeal from Atmore, Alabama, number one draft choice, comes from this little town, 10 kids, and his father once plowed with a mule."

Damn, that sounded pretty good. So, I convinced the paper to let me go to Atmore, Alabama, but the mule was dead. It turned out that Don wasn't even around. His father was there. It was in the evening and he was on the porch swing. He just got in plumbing, and he's pissed off because when the mule died his kids, mainly Don, got him a little riding tractor. He hates it. He wants to get the mule back. I just sat there and talked for a couple of hours, and the next day I came out and met Don.

He took me around to meet the preacher at the church, and showed me the grave where his mother was, and took me to this old lady who was his baby sitter. We just went around town and talked to some of the folks. This town, which is a pretty redneck little town, had made Don its favorite son, which is a little strange for a black fellow. The town was so proud of him they chipped in and bought him a car to drive to the Dolphin camp.

Is that right?

They had a parade for him and the ladies had bake sales on the sidewalks. I just walked around town one day and said, "Look, tell me what you know about Don McNeal." I went in the country-western bars and the dress shop and talked to the mechanics at the garage, and the head of the Chamber of Commerce and everything.

Tell me a little bit about some of your writing habits. You mention that you write slowly. Is that still the case?

That's one criticism of me. I push a deadline right to the last second, and a lot of times go right through it. I've got some poor habits, to be truthful.

Let's hear about them.

First of all, I type with one finger. I can type

about 30 words a minute, or something like that. I come back from a story and make an outline. Sometimes I scribble some of my notes out under different headings. If I were on a real deadline situation, I'd have to break that habit or I'd be in a real jam. My lead sometimes takes me an hour.

You're talking about a formal outline? What does it look like? Is it on a yellow paper or something?

Yes, I get a long legal pad. I write *Intro* at the top. I figure out my lead anecdote. Then I try to think what the main line of the story is. A lot of times I use star lines too. I get two or three different scenes, see the person in the ring, then talk to him later back at his hotel or in the restaurant. Sometime I set two or three different scenes and use star lines.

To cut from one scene to another?

Right. Then I'll just plug along. I write down three or four or five of the best things I have. I'll pop one or two up top, save one for the end, and put one somewhere in the middle so if anything lags, it picks up again. My outline is pretty detailed, even the transitions. I'm going from this idea to that so when I start writing, it's pretty much right there. I've thought the whole story through from A to Z.

OK. You miss deadline. And often your stories are long. I notice a few typos, a few rough spots, a couple of small mistakes, things that might have been picked up by an editor, if he had the time.

I get my copy in late. They can't spend a lot of time on it and I don't proofread enough. Those are poor habits.

OK. I want to ask you about your leads. Your leads are scene setters. Is that something that you strive for every time?

A lot of times, maybe too often. Sometimes I think if I can bring the reader just where I was, it brings him closer to the subject. They can smell them, and taste them, and feel them a little.

Ever receive any criticism, let's say, for putting the main point down low?

Just the other day I heard it. They said, "Read your story on the fight. I had to make the jump before I could tell who won." I have too much drum roll sometimes. Maybe I'm too interested in trying to make some little slice of literature and forget that it's just Joe Blow reading this while he's eating his sandwich at lunch.

Your reputation as a writer has grown. And now you've won an important national award. Has your attitude toward your work changed any?

When I first started writing I thought that everything I wrote ought to be put in bronze someplace. Now, I don't like to read my stories in the paper. I hardly ever do, just because I read them then and I see a little mistake, a typo I made, a little something I could have done differently. I don't go back and read the stories once they come out in the paper. It's just too painful.

H. G. Bissinger
Finalist, Non-Deadline Writing

H. G. BISSINGER, 27, worked as a general assignment and special projects reporter for the *St. Paul Pioneer Press* from 1978-81. While in St. Paul, he wrote a series of stories on a dramatic sky accident and its aftermath, the first part of which is reprinted here. The story was a finalist in this year's competition and is included on the recommendation of David Laventhol, publisher of *Newsday* and chairman of the ASNE writing awards committee. Bissinger was born in New York City and graduated from the University of Pennsylvania with a degree in English in 1976. He has been active in journalism since high school and has covered police, courts, urban affairs, entertainment, and other topics. Bissinger is now a reporter in the Atlantic City bureau of the *Philadelphia Inquirer*.

The plane that fell from the sky

On April 4, 1979, a TWA Boeing 727 bound for Minneapolis-St. Paul suddenly went out of control and rocketed nose down toward the ground at 630 miles an hour. With only precious seconds left before it would have crashed, it miraculously was brought under control. In 44 seconds of terror, the plane fell 34,000 feet. Never has a commercial plane dropped that far that fast and not crashed. For the 82 passengers and seven crew members on board, those 44 seconds became an eternity. And when the ordeal was over, few of their lives would ever be the same.

April 3, 1979
9:35 a.m.
Los Angeles International Airport

The truth was, flying commercial could be boring work. The old philosophy among pilots, starting in the days when the DC-3 was the biggest thing going, was that you didn't really get paid for all the times you flew without a hitch, but for the one time out of a thousand when everything went to hell and you still brought the airplane in. That was the test of skill, and the reason for all the other paychecks.

After 16 years of piloting for Trans World Airlines, 44-year-old Hoot Gibson didn't find his work particularly creative. Or daring. Or exhilarating. After spending 15,709 hours of flight time in the confining cockpits of 727s, DC-9s, and 747s as a flight engineer, co-pilot and captain, things were bound to become as familiar as the boring drone of a jet engine.

Gibson's excitement came when he left the

lumbering commercial birds behind and climbed alone into his own planes to do acrobatic stunts and punch in and out of canyon crevices and clouds.

That kind of airmanship was more in line with his machismo reputation, which, whether it was merited or not, had become the subject of shop talk in TWA hangars and cockpits.

But whatever tidbits circulated about Hoot Gibson's lifestyle, his commercial flying abilities were difficult to fault. In the parlance of his peers, he carried a simple tag: he was a "good airman." He confined his colorful ways to the ground, not the skies.

The April 3 flight package he had drawn was hardly the stuff of glamour, taking him out of Los Angeles at 9:35 a.m. on a hop-skip-and-jump tour to Phoenix, Wichita, Kansas City, Chicago and finally Columbus, Ohio. Once there, Gibson and the other two members of his crew, first officer Scott Kennedy and flight engineer Gary Banks, bedded down for the night in a hotel.

The crew, which had never worked together before, got about eight hours sleep. The next day — April 4 — they left about 3 p.m. for New York's Kennedy Airport.

There was about a two-hour layover at Kennedy as they changed equipment — to Boeing 727-100 aircraft No. N840TW — and prepared for their final hop of the evening.

The plane was old, delivered to TWA in 1965 as part of the first batch of 727s coming out of Boeing's suburban Seattle plant. The destination, considering TWA's other routes, was not the kind of place a pilot would beg for — St. Paul-Minneapolis International on TWA Flight 841.

With all his experience, Hoot Gibson probably could make the trip — a relatively short course over Lake Michigan and Green Bay — with his eyes closed. Any airline pilot could — just get the plane up to cruise altitude and set in the autopilot until it was time to land.

After 15,000 hours of flying, it certainly was not the test of skill that would make a pilot find out just how much he was really worth.

**April 4, 1979
6:55 p.m.
Kennedy International Airport**

Just when it seemed as if there were no alternative except to stay in New York for longer than he wanted to, Bob Reber found TWA Flight 841.

The flight he hoped to get booked on — a Northwest 6 p.m. flight out of LaGuardia — was full. So Reber, 52, walked to the TWA counter at the Sheraton Hotel and the luck there was better: A seat was available on their flight to Minneapolis, leaving at 6:55 p.m.

Typically, the plane was late taking off and did not leave the JFK gate until 7:39 p.m., prompting pilot Hoot Gibson to come on the intercom and give the 82 passengers on board one of those little speeches about being held up.

Eventually, the plane took off at 8:25 p.m. Reber settled into seat 22F, a window seat in the last row of seats in the smoking section, pulled out the copy of the *New York Times* and sipped a cocktail.

The manager of data processing for Powers department stores in the Twin Cities, he stayed wide awake throughout the flight. Falling asleep on planes was a habit he had never acquired. But he thought the trip was extremely dull as airplane flights always are, with the engines humming and the funny smell of disinfectant that tried to rid the cabin of any human smell.

In the *Minneapolis Tribune* that morning, his horoscope by Jeane Dixon had at least been topical for once: "Traveling appeals, but is not favored. Try staying close to home (Cancer.

June 21-July 22)." But Reber didn't pay attention to junk like that.

**April 4, 1979
8:45 p.m.
Nearing the Great Lakes
35,000 feet**

First Officer Scott Kennedy, who had flown the 727 for all but six months of his 13 years at TWA, put the flaps up with effortless routine.

On takeoff, the flaps were extended to produce lift so the plane could get off the ground.

160 Knots. Flaps up from 15 degrees to 5 degrees to increase speed.

190 knots. Flaps up from 5 degrees to 2 degrees.

200 knots. Flaps tucked in all the way.

Flight 841 was cleared by air traffic control to an altitude of 5,000 feet. Then up to 8,000, 23,000, and finally 35,000 feet at 8:45 p.m. The air was calm with a little turbulence — "smooth with a light chop" as the pilots referred to it. Nothing to get excited about.

Five minutes later, the four flight attendants on board, two men, two women, started serving the meal — hot and forgettable food served on plastic trays.

Headwinds of 110 knots were bearing down on Flight 841 as it maintained 35,000 feet altitude. Gibson didn't like that and figured the best way to beat the winds was to go below them — or above them.

At 9:24, Gibson got on the mike with the air traffic control center in Toronto and asked for clearance up to 39,000 feet to beat the winds.

"Centre TW841 like to try Flight Level 390."
"Roger, TW841 climb to maintain FL390."
"Out of 35 for 39."

At 9:38 p.m., Flight 841 reported that it was at 39,000 feet.

"TWA's 841 level 3 nine 0."
"841 roger."

The conditions at that altitude were clear and smooth. It was quiet up there, nice and quiet, the cockpit noise at a whisper compared to other altitudes.

A moonlit trail of clouds shimmered about 4,000 feet below the silver underbelly of the plane as it darted across Michigan in the black night. The clouds stretched for several miles to the shoreline of Lake Michigan, and from his seat in the cockpit, Hoot Gibson could see the on-and-off flicker of distant city lights across the mammoth lake.

At 39,000 feet, the serenity of the sky belonged to Flight 841.

April 4, 1979
9:47 p.m.
Near Saginaw, Michigan
39,619 feet

Dr. Peter Fehr had never particularly liked to fly. To be perfectly honest about it, Fehr used to have a horrendous fear of it, and the whole concept of motion was not something that he had ever quite gotten used to.

As a kid, when he used to go on drives with the family, the result was always the same — he got sick. And his first airplane ride, from Minneapolis to Chicago when he was interviewing to be a missionary in Africa, had left his stomach badly upset.

Fehr, an obstetrician-gynecologist, knew, of course, that it was impossible to live in the modern world without flying. So, with the help of God and large dosages of Dramamine, he had persevered. He made it to Africa as a missionary, suffering in ancient DC-3s that barely wobbled over the African swamps, making so much noise that it sounded like the metal was being sheared off.

But for the past 11 years that Fehr had lived in Minneapolis, things changed. He had been able to get on an airplane whenever it was required. For the past year, in fact, he had been flying without fear and without Dramamine.

But it still didn't take much to get unnerved. A few days earlier, when he had been on his way to New York for a convention, the woman sitting next to him, a large Italian woman, kept repeating her rosary and kissing her prayer book.

Fehr had an urge to look her straight in the eye and say, "Lady, these planes keep flying and most of 'em don't go down." A timid man, he didn't have the courage to say it. But, of course, he was right. The trip to New York was without consequence.

Fehr went to his convention at the New York Hilton, and now he was returning home on Flight 841.

The seat belt sign had gone off, dinner had been served, and the food trays picked up. It was time to relax.

Fehr and the man sitting next to him, a University of Minnesota professor, chatted for a bit.

Suddenly, without warning, the plane shuddered and began to feel as though it were sliding sideways across the sky. There was the sensation that the plane was changing speed and maybe even trying to land. But at 39,000 feet?

"We can't be in Minneapolis already?" said the professor.

Fehr knew the professor was right.

**April 4, 1979
9:47.57 p.m.
Near Saginaw
39,046 feet**

Gary Bank's mind idled.

There wasn't much for the flight engineer to do, so he started filling out parts of his log and looked vacantly at the array of instruments and switches before him. Then he felt a high frequency vibration.

Co-pilot Kennedy was preoccupied with trying to figure out the plane's ground speed.

And Hoot Gibson, with the plane set on autopilot and flying steady, put away his charts and cleaned up the cockpit.

Then he heard a sound — a slight buzz — and saw the wheel of the airplane turning slowly to the left, about 10 degrees. The plane was turning to the right for some reason and the autopilot was trying to correct it.

The buzz continued, and now the plane was shaking slightly. And it was turning slightly, and still rolling to the right. And the autopilot was still turning the wheel to the left. But it wasn't doing a thing. The plane was still turning to the right.

Gibson watched for about 10 seconds. Then he disconnected the autopilot. The plane was still rolling to the right. Still rolling.

Gibson grabbed onto the wheel with both hands and turned it all the way to the left. Leaning back in his seat, he took his foot and punched down on the rudder pedal all the way to the left to try to bring the plane around.

It did nothing. The thing was still going to the right. Through 20 degrees. Then 30.

Speaking to his co-pilot, he said what was by now the inevitable truth.

"This airplane's going over."

It continued.

50 degrees.

60 degrees.

70 degrees.

And in that fraction of a second, Hoot Gibson felt stark terror. The plane was rolling over and going in. He knew it. That was it.

He was going to die. And take 88 other people down with him.

April 4, 1979
9:48.04 p.m.
Near Saginaw
36,307 feet

The tiny 2-month-old baby in Holly Wicker's lap started gasping for breath and turning blue as the plane hurtled downward at a vertical pitch, the speed increasing.

The baby's name was Asha (it means "hope" in Hindi) and this was her first experience in the United States after coming from India. She was on her way to Minneapolis to be adopted and Holly was in charge of her.

With each foot that the plane lost, the forces of gravity (G forces) increased. The pressure was forcing Wicker back into her seat, shoving her skin backwards, almost like someone had grabbed her cheeks and was trying to pull them back to see how much they would stretch.

Wicker tried to rotate Asha onto her back and pull the baby toward her. But she couldn't — the gravity was too great — and instead Wicker leaned forward.

Out of the corner of her eye, she looked across the aisle and saw the instrument panels over the passenger's heads pop down even though they weren't supposed to — forcing down oxygen masks and light bulbs and wires.

Wicker watched the knuckles of hands turning white as passengers tried to fight gravity and reach for the masks. She watched people with their mouths open as though they were trying to scream. But there wasn't a sound, as though the gravity had frozen their cries.

Wicker bent down and gave Asha a breath. She gave another. And then another, when a searing pain ripped across her chest. She couldn't give anymore. There was nothing left. And she knew that the next breath she would take would have to be for herself — not for the tiny baby on her lap turning blue.

April 4, 1979
9:48.07 p.m.
Near Saginaw
34,459 feet

The plane went into its first roll and Gibson pulled back on the control wheel to try to apply enough downward pressure to keep the passengers in their seats. With the seat belt sign off, they all could be walking around for all he knew.

He closed off the engine throttles — shutting off some of the power to the plane's engines — and started saying "Get 'em up. Get 'em up here." Kennedy thought he was talking to the plane, as pilots often do, trying to coax it back up, pleading with it.

But what Gibson wanted was for Kennedy to grab the "spoiler" handle and pull it back so the flaps on the top of the wing would pop up and help slow the plane down.

By now the plane was into a second roll — this one almost vertical. Gibson let go of the control wheel and pulled the spoiler handle up and down himself.

Nothing happened.

He tugged on the control wheel to see if he could get the plane to reduce its pitch.

It didn't matter.

The plane was in a dive.

By this time, Gary Banks had pulled his seat in between Gibson and Kennedy and tried to get a fix on their instruments. He couldn't figure out what was going on and he needed to get a look at the artificial horizon indicator — an instrument that tells a plane's position on the horizon and where it is pointing. It is divided into two colors — blue for the sky and black for the ground.

Gibson's elbow was blocking the indicator. So Banks looked over at Kennedy's panel, which has an identical set of instruments.

The indicator was black. Pure black. Not a trace of blue in there. It was like walking into a room and finding all the furniture on the ceiling. Banks couldn't believe what he was seeing. And it meant only one thing.

The plane was heading straight for the ground nose down.

He watched as Gibson and Kennedy tried to regain control. From his days as an Air Force instructor on the supersonic T-38s, where you did spiral dives on purpose just to let the student know what the plane could and couldn't do, Banks was impressed: Gibson and Kennedy were doing everything right.

But they weren't saving the plane. They weren't doing it.

Banks glanced at Gibson. He glanced to the right at Kennedy. Then he sat back in his chair and became very calm. He knew the ending now, and in a whisper he confirmed it to himself:

"It is all over. I wonder what it's gonna feel like to hit the ground."

April 4, 1979
9:48.10 p.m.
Near Saginaw
29,982 feet

The increasing gravity forces pulled Peter Fehr's glasses off his face. He tried to grab them with his arms but he couldn't — gravity had glued them to the armrests. The upper part of his body went upright against his seat like a diving board.

The plane was rattling like crazy, the vibration increasing with each foot of the plunge. The noise sounded like the B-29s that went down in the World War II movies, that horrible, moaning whine that got louder and louder. And then there was another sound, the wrenching, gnarling sound of metal being torn from the right wing.

Fehr knew there was no way the pilot — *any pilot* — was going to bring the plane back up.

The passenger in the seat in front of him kept trying to coax the plane back up. It sounded like he was talking to the pilot. "Take it easy," the man whispered. "You haven't lost it yet. You can pull it out." Fehr thought the man was a fool.

He knew he was going to die.

He became calm and objective. The scene became an abstraction, with Fehr a detached observer.

In the remaining seconds left, he began to make a checklist. He reviewed his will — it was in order and his wife should be well-cared for. He remembered what he had said to his four kids before he left for New York.

And it irked him now that one of his sons had taken out a loan to buy a new pair of tires for his car without coming to him. The interest rates were probably ridiculous...his son was probably getting gouged to death...it wasn't a good business deal...in fact, it was downright stupid...why did he do something like that...they should have talked about it beforehand...they really should have.

The roar of the plane grew louder.

April 4, 1979
9:48.16 p.m.
Near Saginaw
24,121 feet

As the descent of the plane grew faster, Scott Kennedy's mind worked faster.

He remembered the crash of a commercial plane that had been flying at 39,000 feet and dropped into Lake Michigan.

He remembered the crash of the Pacific Southwest Airlines jet in San Diego that had happened only six months ago and left close to 150 people dead.

And then he remembered a conversation he had with the flight engineer only the night before — an insider's conversation about recovering a plane from a vertical stall.

From his experience in the Air Force, Banks knew of only one way to do it — pop the drag shoot on the tail of the plane — a parachute-type piece of equipment that was normally used to slow the aircraft down during landing. Activating it during a stall would slow the plane down enough so the pilot could get control of it back, Banks had told Kennedy.

The co-pilot watched as Gibson tried just

about every maneuver there was and still the plane was screaming through the sky. He was impressed by Gibson's perseverance, his reluctance to give up.

Then Kennedy's eye was drawn to something that might help — putting the landing gear down.

He suggested that to Gibson and had his hand poised and waiting on the landing gear handle. The plane continued to plummet, the altimeter unwinding so fast that no one in the cockpit could read it.

21,000 feet.

18,000 feet.

They were getting close and Gibson could see the lights of cities spinning through the fog.

15,000 feet and dropping vertical.

"Gear down," said Gibson

Kennedy followed the command.

For a second, the two pilots fought against each other as they worked their control wheels — Gibson pushing in to get the tail into the wind current so it would fly again, Kennedy pulling his out to keep the nose of the plane up.

The gear dropped down.

The explosion was deafening, like nothing Gibson or Kennedy or Banks had ever heard in their lives.

TWA Flight 841 continued to fall.

10,000 feet.

8,000 feet.

Gibson didn't know where he was. He couldn't read the instruments. Where the hell was the ground?

And then the plane started to fly again.

And Gibson couldn't help but feel what a damn shame it was that he was getting control back just as the plane was going to crack.

He pulled back on the control wheel as if he was trying to rein a wild mustang. The nose of the plane shot up about 50 degrees. Gibson almost looped the plane he was so desperate to avoid the Michigan farmland beneath him. He was afraid the wings might move, or snap off the plane, but he had no choice but to pull up.

The G forces were incredible — flight data showed them registering 6 at one point — meaning a person's weight was six times what it normally would be. The blood rushed downward from the brain as passengers were flattened into their seats with incredible force. Their faces were pushed sideways as though they were being held in a vise.

Gibson, the acrobatic pilot, had taken 6 Gs before and knew what they were like. Banks, as he had learned in the Air Force, tightened his stomach and tried to keep the blood from pushing down.

The nose still pointed up about 50 degrees as the plane punched through the clouds again — this time on the way up.

Banks felt a rush of panic. If Gibson pulled the nose of the plane down too fast to bring it level, the reverse force of the gravity could be enough to rip an engine off its mount.

Banks coaxed Gibson to get the wings level and gently ease the nose over. "Keep 'em level," he repeated, "Keep 'em level."

Gibson was having trouble figuring out the plane's direction. And then he saw the moon. He pinned it on the windshield, it became his compass, and he kept it in the same exact spot until he pushed the nose over and brought the plane level.

The noise and vibration in the tiny cockpit was incredible. Almost unbearable. Inside the cabin, the shaking and gravity had caused more of the overhead panels to pop open. Oxygen masks accidentally came tumbling down in some of the rows. But some of the passengers didn't realize it was an accident. They thought everyone was supposed to have a mask. And they were clawing at their closed panels with their fingers, trying to pry them open.

Gibson got on the intercom. He had to say *something*. Anything.

"We've had a slight problem, but everything seems to be under control."

April 4, 1979
9:51 p.m.
Near Saginaw
10,509 feet

Even though the plane was flying again, Atul Bhatt knew something was terribly wrong. One look at the flight attendants told him that.

They were agitated, upset, one of them was crying. And he was scared to death. Once when he was 10 years old, he was riding his bicycle on the edge of a highway when he lost control and fell under a moving truck. The driver just caught a glimpse of him, and the back wheels came to a halt right next to his body.

He had missed death by a screeching second. But he had been a kid then, and the whole thing had happened so quickly.

But this wasn't happening quickly. This was taking forever. There was time — too much time — to think again and again about what would happen. As the plane had started to plummet, the knowledge of a death that would be quick and painless had somehow been comforting.

But now the plane was going to make a crash landing, and Bhatt didn't even know where it would be. The Chicago airport maybe? Or a forest? Or a farm? It was so dark outside, he couldn't see a thing.

The fear of being paralyzed gnawed at him. Or of being maimed. Or half-burned. And Bhatt, 27, a Ph.D. candidate from India at the University of Minnesota, couldn't bear that. If the plane did crash, he wanted to die quickly. Survival at any odds, with a thousand different possible after effects, wasn't worth the risk.

But the choice wasn't his.

Bhatt was lost in his fear when an Italian woman sitting next to him, after watching his agony for a few minutes now, spoke up. "Don't be scared, young man," said the woman.

Bhatt felt a little embarrassed after that. Here he was a grown man, being admonished just like a little kid for being a coward — not even tough enough to take a bumpy little plane ride. And then he thought a little more.

And he knew in his heart exactly how he felt.

And he couldn't think of one single reason to be brave about it.

He had never been more scared in his entire life.

Dive of Flight 841

Seconds Elapsed	Altitude Loss	MPH*	G Forces**
0	—	513	1.27
1.3	224	508	1.46
3.5	1,045	520	1.65
6.9	2,739	540	1.92
9.7	4,587	580	1.75
14.0	9,064	631	2.16
19.8	14,925	610	3.68
31.2	20,959	576	3.69
42.6	29.036	575	4.76
44.3	34,118	552	5.25

*Miles per hour is estimated.
**G force is a measure of gravity. G force of 1 is normal. For example, G Force of 5 means that a person's body weight is five times what it normally should be.

Source: Flight 841 Data Recorder

April 4, 1979
9:55 p.m.
60 miles from Detroit, Michigan
12,749 feet

Hoot Gibson needed to find an airport. Quickly.

He checked with air traffic control about Saginaw, where the weather was overcast with light snow and three miles visibility. Then he checked Lansing. And Detroit, where the weather was a little better but certainly not perfect — overcast skies, seven miles visibility, wind at 10 knots.

Although it was the farthest away of the three choices — about 60 miles — Detroit's Metro Airport seemed to Gibson to be the most logical choice. He was familiar with the airport and it could handle a major emergency.

And he figured he could make it.

While Gibson handled the controls of the plane. Kennedy and Banks went through a series of emergency "checklists" to pinpoint what was wrong with the plane and how to try to remedy it.

The noise and vibrating inside the cockpit was still deafening. Banks and Kennedy were shouting, and they still could barely understand each other and had to rely on reading lips.

The diagnosis was not good.

One of the plane's hydraulic power systems was out, so the flaps would have to be extended by an alternate power source. A yaw damper — an electronic device on the rudder that stops a plane from weaving uncontrollably — was apparently out of commission, too.

The landing gear indicator lights inside the cockpit were red, meaning the dropped gear was unlocked and unsafe to land on. It would have to be cranked down manually.

Banks hands shook and his body shivered

as he removed a plate from the floor of the cockpit and used a lever to put the main landing gear down by hand. There was no feel on the gear at all, as though it wasn't holding. And when he was through, the indicator lights still were red.

The nose landing gear was extended manually, and the indicator light showed green — the gear was down and locked into place. Once the nose gear dropped, the terrible cockpit noise stopped. Banks couldn't believe what a relief it was to have a little quiet. That noise had almost driven him crazy.

The crew then tried to use alternate power to get the flaps to extend, so the plane would slow down and be easier to land.

The flaps were barely out before the aircraft rolled sharply to the left. Gibson couldn't believe it — he figured he had lost the plane again. But he recovered, and for the rest of the trip he had to fly with the control wheel and the rudder pedal pushed all the way to the right so the plane would not roll over.

Gibson realized that his margin for error here was very small. Below about 170 knots an hour, the plane would begin to roll. Above about 210 knots an hour, the same thing would happen. It gave him about 40 knots to work with, and the likelihood of a landing under the worst possible conditions.

When TWA Flight 841 came in to Detroit on runway 3L, it would be making its touchdown at almost twice the normal speed. And on landing gear that, for all Hoot Gibson knew, might not even be there.

**April 4, 1979
10 p.m.
Near Detroit
13,000 feet**

Passenger Barbara Merrill had crashed to the floor trapped in the lavatory. Stewardess Fran Schaller, walking to the liquor cart to get someone a drink, had fallen flat in the middle of the aisle. Unable to get up, a passenger cradled her head while she clung to the cart with her left hand. Others on board had blacked out.

As the plane leveled out, Merrill, 41, crawled out of the bathroom and made it as far as the right aisle seat in the last row of the plane, Row 22.

Her ribs ached, maybe one of them was cracked. Her hip had crashed against the toilet seat when she had been thrown to the floor, and she had a cut on her knee.

Merrill's 14-year-old daughter, Susan, walked to the back of the cabin to be with her mother.

She sat in seat 22E, in between her mother and Bob Reber.

Under the conditions, there couldn't have

been a more reassuring figure. Reber had blacked out almost instantly after the plane had started to dive. But now he felt quite calm and not really aware that something terrible had happened — or was going to happen.

"We're gonna die!" Reber heard Mrs. Merrill repeat over and over. "We're gonna die!"

"Are we?" Mrs. Merrill's daughter asked, her mother's sense of panic becoming infectious.

Reber remained immune. "Don't worry about it," he told them. "If you get to pick your place to land, you got a 50-50 chance."

April 4, 1979
10:20 p.m.
Flying over Detroit Metro Airport
1,600 feet

Gary Banks called flight attendant Mark Moscicki into the cockpit and asked him if he remembered his training for an emergency landing.

"You have 10 minutes to get the plane ready, and you get back here in eight minutes," Banks told him.

Moscicki met briefly with the three other flight attendants in the center galley. Then they went to work.

They whipped through the cabin, instructing passengers to remove their glasses, pens, high-heeled shoes, false teeth, canes, anything that was sharp and might cause injury.

The started emptying the overhead racks, distributing available pillows and blankets. One of the stewardesses threw Catherine Rascher's leather jacket on the floor, and she winced. Even in a time of fear and crises, it was hard for her to forget the coat was brand new and cost $200.

A passenger got into an argument with a

flight attendant who wanted to remove his glasses. The passenger refused. The attendant persisted, and finally just plucked the glasses off the man's face.

Another passenger willingly had her glasses removed, but gave forewarning that she was blind without them. The flight attendant immediately designated the man sitting directly behind her as her guardian: The woman's life and the lives of her two children depended upon him, the man was told.

Moscicki got on the intercom and told the passengers about the plane's evacuation procedures. He showed them the impact position — hands behind the head, the body bent forward as far as it would go, a pillow to cushion the head from the seat in front.

At 1,600 feet, Gibson flew over the Detroit airport tower so ground personnel could get a look at the landing gear. Searchlights panned the underbelly of the plane. From what they could tell, the gear looked down and locked.

Peeking out the windows from the emergency position, passengers could see a mass of fire trucks sitting on the runway, waiting to see whether TWA Flight 841 would make it. The plane swooped so low that they could see the expressions on the firemen's faces.

After the fly-by, Banks opened the cockpit door to speak to the flight attendants one more time. But when he glimpsed outside, he saw everybody bent over, ready for the plane to crash.

The action was a little premature, there was still a little time left, so Banks got on the intercom and told everybody to sit easy for a moment. He said he would tell them when it was time to assume the ... he was about to say "crash position" but then he stopped himself and just told the passengers he would let them know when it was time to get ready.

Gibson circled on the final approach to the runway.

He turned the plane downwind, his eyes

glued to the strip so he wouldn't lose track of it for a second.

Suddenly, the plane started rolling to the left again.

Gibson was losing control, the plane was getting away from him again.

The crew erupted in the cockpit. After 40 minutes of fighting to keep the aircraft up, the adrenaline was running out. Now was the perfect time to screw up.

"Don't let it roll too far!" yelled Banks, on the verge of panic, "Don't let it roll!"

Kennedy got on the control wheel and started working the engine throttles. He cut the power to the right engine and increased the power to the left.

Moments away from landing, TWA Flight 841 skidded level.

April 4, 1979
10:30 p.m.
On approach to Detroit Metro Airport
50 feet

Frederick and Catherine Rascher held hands and waited.

They had been married for 43 years, had just enjoyed a wonderful trip to Spain, and were looking forward to a life of quiet retirement in St. Paul. Whatever happened now, at least, they would be together.

The turned and looked at each other as they prepared for the crash landing.

"We've had a nice life together," said Mrs. Rascher.

"It's too bad it has to end this way," said her husband.

The plane was on its approach now. Lifting his head up slightly, Frederick Rascher peeked out the window and began the final countdown.

"Forty feet ... thirty feet ... twenty feet ... ten feet ... get ready."

They bent their heads down and waited for the last time.

April 4, 1979
10:31 p.m.
Landing at Detroit Metro Airport

Gibson bore down on the runway at 170 knots. As he was coming in, the plane started again to roll to the left. The left landing gear hit the runway first — "pretty damn smooth" Gibson thought to himself — and the gear was holding.

The plane was rolling quite a bit and Gibson had to get the right gear on the runway, although he thought the gear would probably shear off on impact.

He brought the plane level and the right gear wasn't even hitting. Maybe it already had fallen off, Gibson thought.

The gear, when it had been extended during the dive, had broken its side brace. If any substantial pressure was put on it from either side, it would collapse on impact.

Using his controls, Gibson tilted the right wing down and finally the right gear hit the runway. It was there...and it was holding.

A burst of applause went up from the passengers as the plane touched down. Hoot Gibson was getting a sitting ovation.

Part of the right gear dragged along the runway, causing sparks as Gibson turned left toward the emergency vehicles. As soon as the plane stopped, fire engines sped up and started spraying the aircraft with foam.

Gibson felt exhausted — more exhausted perhaps than he had ever been in his entire life. He also felt relieved and surprised. From 39,000 feet until touchdown some 43 minutes later, he had been convinced that the plane was going to crash.

The only thing he hadn't figured out was where.

**April 4, 1979
10:40 p.m.
On the ground at Detroit Metro Airport**

Dr. Peter Fehr thought one of the passengers on board was having a heart attack.

He got an oxygen tank for her and made sure she got to a hospital. He gave medical attention to some of the other passengers. And then, once outside the plane, Peter Fehr — the cool, detached doctor —lost control. For 20 minutes he vomited and wretched and his legs turned to water. Then he called home to tell his family he was safe.

* * *

Atul Bhatt looked over at the man in his row and couldn't believe what he was seeing. The plane had landed, it was probably about to blow up, there were firemen all over the place, and here was this guy whose first instinct wasn't to run for his life, or move quickly, or even to move at all. Instead he slowly took his comb out of his pocket and started combing his hair.

Bhatt had no pretentions of vanity. In his eagerness to get off the plane, he left his suit jacket on board. And when a bottle of Scotch was passed around in the shivering cold of the runway, he gladly swigged.

* * *

The passenger came up to Gary Banks as he and the other crew members were leaving the cockpit.

"Isn't it interesting?" the man said.

Interesting? What the hell was interesting about a plane that by all rights should have been a hole in the ground and left 89 people dead?

"God no!" said Banks, slightly stunned by the comment.

But the passenger wasn't finished.

"Isn't it interesting that it isn't anyone's time on this plane to die," said the man. And then he walked away.

(H.G. Bissinger wrote two more major parts to this story: "The Aftermath," which describes the effects of the accident on the passengers and crew; and "The Investigation," which chronicles the official inquiries into the cause of the accident. He also wrote a sidebar on the character and career of pilot Hoot Gibson.)

Observations and questions

1) We applied a rigorous test to H. G. Bissinger's work, and it stood up admirably. We gave a copy of "The Plane That Fell from the Sky" to Peter A. Selkey, a Delta pilot who lives in St. Petersburg. We asked him to read the story and to comment on its technical accuracy. Selkey suggested a place in the story where Bissinger might clarify his description of *pitch*. But Selkey concluded that the piece is technically correct in every instance. Most newspaper stories about airplane crashes are written under pressure and contain errors, he said, but this story is technically accurate.

2) The subheadline reveals that the plane did not crash. The news event was more than a year old and generally known to Bissinger's audience. Although the reader has some idea of the outcome, this story has all the elements of suspense that one might expect from a novel or adventure movie. Examine the story and discuss how Bissinger uses narrative to create suspense.

3) Examine the opening of Bissinger's story. It is rather laid back compared to the adventure to come. In fact, the author uses a recurring motif in which the ordinary, boring ritual of flying is shattered by a frightening, extraordinary event. Study this technique and discuss its effect on the reader.

4) The writer carefully manipulates points of view. Examine the events through the eyes of different characters. How does the information provided by each character give us a more complete picture of the event?

5) Notice how Bissinger shifts the perspective of the story from cockpit to cabin. Next time you are on an airplane, take notes about everything you can see and hear. Also consider how the flight attendants and the cockpit crew have different perspectives on the events of the flight than do you. Also consider the perspectives of people sitting in different parts of the cabin. Get someone to give you a tour of a cockpit.

6) Bissinger had to make sense of the technical language of aviation, something he knew little about. Make believe you are editing his copy. Look at the descriptions of technical areas — things like *G force, vertical roll,* and *pitch*. Are there things that the reader might not understand or that are inadequately explained?

7) What function is served by the section dividers that recount date, time and location? Does Bissinger need to repeat April 4 so many times? What effect is he trying to create in so doing?

8) Notice how understated Bissinger's style is. Is such a lean style appropriate for such an extraordinary event? Be his editor. Conduct a search and destroy mission for any unnecessary adjectives and adverbs. Look at your own work and seek to eliminate unnecessary modifiers.

9) From film and fiction you probably have some notions of how sky disasters go. How does this non-fiction account correspond to your notions?

10) Read *The Right Stuff* by Tom Wolfe (New York: Farrar. Straus. Giroux, 1979). Especially read pp. 44-78 in which Wolfe describes the character of the famous test pilot Chuck Yeager. Compare and contrast Wolfe's treatment of Yeager to Bissinger's characterization of Hoot Gibson.

11) Discuss the use of attribution in this story. It is used sparingly. Has the writer convinced

you to trust him on the matter of attribution, or would you have liked to see more evidence of where certain bits of information came from?

12) Notice Bissinger's use of quotations. He is most selective. Do you think that was a wise decision, or are there places where you would have rather heard more from the characters on the airplane?

A conversation with
H.G. Bissinger

CLARK: I see that you were a general assignment and special projects reporter in St. Paul for three years. Is that how you got involved in this story?

BISSINGER: I had been on the paper about four or five months, and when this broke as a news story, I was assigned to do it. I did it, and it stuck in my mind. I just felt that to do it as a spot news story was fine but there was something much more there.

Actually, two years later my wife said she thought it would be interesting to see what happened to the people on this plane. I said yes, I think that's a pretty good idea. It evolved from there, and I knew after the first two interviews that this was something very, very special. It was worth as much time as I could get. I immediately wrote a proposal to the editors, and they said go with it and take as much time as you need.

So you have an event that's actually two years old?

Right.

The reporting of this interests me. How did you proceed from there?

Well, first I pulled out all the clips. I wanted to get the names of passengers. It stuck in my mind that about three weeks after the incident the Associated Press had done a story about some of the passengers' immediate aftereffects. I carted it out and saw names of people who were from the Minneapolis-St. Paul area. Then

I just got on the phone.
　　I found two women and interviewed them. Their lawyer happened to be a plane buff. His firm specialized in airplane litigation, and he had all the government investigative material. He was more than willing to share it with me.
　　I went through court records because I wanted to see who had filed suit. I had assumed that with something like this people would file suit. I guess there were six or seven suits, and then it just fell in place. The lawyer was key because he had all the depositions, all the government material that I was able to lay out. After seeing the material, I realized I would be able to do a good re-enactment.

Go over this again with me. This was a lawyer for two of the women?

Right. He was representing two of the women in a personal injury suit.

And what sort of information did he have?

Cases like this were investigated by the National Transportation Safety Board, and he had gotten all the public records. But the nice thing was that he had it all in Minneapolis. He had all the information that had been compiled, the original depositions that were taken, various investigative reports, the chronology on these flight data recorders. They do it in tenth-of-a-second splits and that's how I was able to head each section down to a second. They were very, very closely delineated. It took me about three or four days just to go through them for the first time.

Describe that for me again because that is such an important structural device in the piece. What is this thing that breaks it down?

Every plane has a flight data recorder, every commercial plane. They are really there in case of accidents.

This is not the Black Box?

It actually is the Black Box, and they keep it in the tail of the plane in case there is a crash. In the Air Florida crash, you remember, they were searching for the Black Box and were unable to find it. This plane had one, too, and by some mechanical device they are able to keep tenth-of-second splits as to what happened.

It would have some time device and would also keep track of things like altitude and that sort of thing?

It keeps altitude, speed and distance. It would record how far the plane fell between, say, one second, three seconds, and five seconds, things like that.

Have they taken that and transcribed that?

Yes. They basically made a chronological printout.

OK. That explains a lot of interesting things to me. Now tell me about the human side of it. What sort of interviewing did you have to do and at what point?

The first interview I did was with these two women. One interesting thing about this event, people remembered virtually everything they had done that day, and I really didn't have a bad interview. And throughout the story there was only one person who did not want to talk to me. There was one girl who said it was just too emotionally stirring for her to talk. Everyone else was more than willing to talk and to share whatever material they had compiled.

A lot of people had kept their own scrapbooks. They kept their tickets. They kept everything — which was a wonderful source of information. I used that tremendously. And so I started with these two interviews and they worked very well.

How many passengers did you interview?

I am guessing. I'd say I interviewed between 15 and 20 passengers.

Most living around your area?

Virtually all of them. There was one who was not. I think he was from Connecticut. All were living in the area, and so I think in all but one case they were personal interviews, probably each lasting anywhere between two and three hours.

OK. During the process of the interviews, what sort of information were you trying to derive? Did you have, at this point, a perception of what the story would look like? Had you made the decision about chronology?

I knew after the second week that what I wanted to do was this three-part structure. I wanted to do the reconstruction, and I wanted to do the aftermath, and then I wanted to get into the government investigation. That sort of directed the interviews. Not only did I want to find out what had happened to them afterward, but I also wanted to find out, as precisely as I could, what had happened to them on the plane. As I say, they all seemed to have pretty remarkable memories. Details were obviously very, very important. I think that was the key to the first part.

Now your chronology from the data recorder has been precisely drawn. How was

it possible for you, in the course of interviewing, to match the perceptions and experiences of individual passengers to your chronology? Did you have those key markers of time, like the first time when the plane started to roll and that sort of thing? How did that work out?

During an investigation they take the information on the data recorder and then, not only do they make a printout of it, they write up reports which correlate what happened to the plane at a given time. They break it down into tenths of a second. So that is how it would correlate to the passengers. They would describe what was happening. Then I could go back over these various reports and pinpoint it. They also keep communication between the cockpit and the control tower. They keep it on the same page with the printout of the flight data information, so you are able to correlate it that way.

I see. Maybe if you could give me a specific example just to make it clear to me. Let's say you were interviewing the doctor, and you are talking to him about his experience of taking the flight, just sitting there having his drink or whatever, and suddenly being aware of something wrong. Then you would be able to match that up to things that were happening in the cockpit and other data you have put together.

Right. You know, he described the plane as sort of shuddering, a shuddering effect like it was trying to land. In the investigative reports, I forget what the time was, it was at such and such a second, such and such a time, the plane began a kind of "buffeting effect," they called it. That happened at a precise second, at a precise time, and they were able to correlate it that way.

At some point did you write an outline or a chart or something to keep all these things straight?

I never wrote an outline. I usually don't do that. I think it restrains the writing process. I just kept legal pad notebooks. I had about five notebooks, and I had all the investigative material. I went back and forth to it constantly. It just seemed to come together. I probably spent about a month to a month-and-a-half on the reporting, and the writing took a month. It was the longest time I've ever spent writing anything. Obviously, during the course of writing I would have to go back and try to pinpoint what was happening in each time frame.

So you spent the first month immersing yourself in the material before facing any of the specific writing problems?

Right.

In retrospect, what were your major writing problems, what were the trickiest parts?

The hardest part was not to overwrite. I think all journalists want to show how well they can write and make it very descriptive and flowing, which is important. I think in the first section someone read it and commented, "It doesn't have an adjective in it." And I think that is true. The hardest thing was to be restrained and let the story tell itself, almost in a flat tone. It has such an inherent drama to it that to go one step further and inject too many descriptive phrases would have damaged it.

Isn't there a tradition of understatement among airline pilots? When Gibson comes back on the intercom after this incredible event, he says, "We have a little problem

here." I thought that linked up very well to what you were trying to accomplish.

Right. Exactly. I just wanted the events to sort of unfold by themselves. I almost tell myself I am kind of a river guide, or almost in a sense describing an operation. The other hard part was dealing with a lot of technical detail.

The key was to bring the reader inside an airplane. When you think about it, airplanes are one of the most universally used technological tools in the world. Everyone has taken an airplane and virtually no one has any idea of how an airplane works. They particularly never get inside a cockpit. And so getting inside the cockpit for me was crucially important and to describe, without being too analytical or too technological, what exactly was happening.

I guess that is both a reporting and a writing problem. As far as reporting is concerned did you have any expert that you could rely upon to help you to translate technical information?

I did, and I was very fortunate. I think it is something that good journalists do and should do more of. I was able to use the facilities in the Twin Cities which have two major airlines headquartered there, and also a commission that oversees the metropolitan airports. I probably met with their executives on four or five occasions to go over material, to explain to me what this meant, what was happening.

I also called up Republic Airlines, and I said I would like to get a tour of a 727 from top to bottom, go inside a cockpit. I wanted them to show me what the slats are, show me what the flaps are, show me what the various buttons are. So I got up one morning at 5:30 and went to one of their hangars. And there was a 727 there, and one of their engineers gave me an hour-long tour, so I could become familiar with this huge technological device that I was trying to describe, and obviously had never piloted.

This lawyer is a private pilot. I went up with him in a plane for an hour so he could show me what happens when you do this, and this is what the plane appeared to do, and this is how a stall works.

In retrospect, have those details held up? Has anyone come to you and questioned whether the technical information was exactly right?

No one has questioned it. I know the pilots, after reading the story, said the information as far as they were concerned was pretty much technically right, down to the very last detail.

Certainly during the course of writing the story, if there was something that I didn't understand or something that simply seemed implausible, I would check with various sources. If this is plausible, can this work this way? They would say yes or say well something may be screwed up. Check it back.

You probably had an advantage in having to ask some naive questions about how things work because, I presume, your readers would have some of the same questions.

Exactly.

So, in the writing of it, what did you do? Did you just make a conscious decision to avoid using any technical language that would raise unnecessary questions?

I wanted to have as much technical information as I could, but at the same time, I wanted to explain it in a way that people could understand it. A lot of the reporting was trying to understand this information either conceptually or visually by taking a tour of a 727 or going up in a plane or reading one of the latest textbooks so I can try to understand the process. A lot of rewriting was involved. The editor would say, "I don't understand this, and I'm sure the reader is not going to understand it." So I'd have to write it in such a way that everyone would understand it.

I presume many readers would be familiar with the story. How were you able to create suspense in a story where many readers knew the outcome?

I like to let a story unfold. The lead graph in which you tell everything all at once, I think that takes away a lot of the inherent drama. In this story, I felt the way to do it was to start slow, have a kind of dramatic buildup. The lead in which Gibson and others say, "Fine," and it gets pretty damn boring, and nothing very exciting happens.

In many ways it's like monitoring a nuclear plant. You are there in case something crazy breaks and you do your job. This was a mundane flight like any other in which a passenger is in New York on business and wants to get home and he has the typical hassles and he can't get the flight he wants, and he gets a flight and he's got his *New York Times*, and finally gets a seat, and all he wants is a drink, and wants to relax.

And he starts falling from the sky?

Right. And also to get inside the cockpit to give readers a sense of how the plane works, that the flaps go up the various degrees, increments, but it's all very, very routine and this is a flight like any other except for 44 seconds, and then everyone is turned topsy turvy. I really had to pull back the reins, and try not to go too much the other way where people say, "Well, it's too dead, dull."

Let me ask you this. Did you tell me that you wrote the first news story about this?

Right.

OK. Now, what sort of a lead did you have on that? Do you remember?

It was a soft lead. The incident happened very late, April 4th. So it didn't come over the wires until the following day. So I was writing for the April 6, 1979, paper. To me, I felt that to write a lead saying a 727 dropped 34,000 feet, or whatever, and to write that kind of hard news lead, I felt even then would really not get any sense of what happened. This was an incredible event. When you talk to people on airplanes, there is nothing more terrifying than being in that situation where you really don't know what has happened. So I led with a woman who was from the Minneapolis area who was trapped in the bathroom.

OK. Let me ask you a philosophical question because it is something that is being talked about a lot. How do you answer the charge, "Well, people don't have the time to try to figure out what you want to tell them. The writer has a responsibility to get the news as high up in the story as possible?" What do you think of that sort of criticism?

Well, I think it's a nice generalization. To start with a lead in which you are describing the true and sheer terror of a passenger who was locked in a bathroom and is being banged around and falling to the floor and can't get up because the gravity forces are so intense. That's news. That's what people want to read. It wasn't a lead in which I spent four or five graphs telling about the marvels of air transportation, the jet age, or something like that.

OK. So what you are saying is that even if you take an indirect lead, you're still trying to give the reader an understanding of the full significance of the event, and a reason to continue reading.

Exactly. I think by using a soft lead for that original news story, I am getting to the heart of the story as opposed to flitting around. And there is a problem in that. I do see that kind of showboating in journalists telling the reader I am going to show you how well I can write, how well I can put together phrases before we get to the root of the matter.

Considering its length, I think the first part of the story pretty much gets to the heart of things very quickly and with the headings for each section you know exactly where you are.

Actually, I remember in the original version I had dwelled probably for four or five or six more graphs on Gibson's personality, which I found fascinating, and it's kind of an intrinsic part of the story. In retrospect, I think it was a wise decision to delete that. Of course when editors make decisions initially, you never think they're wise. But my editor said no, it's too much. Get to the story, we can talk about Gibson's personality later, and she was right.

It's one of those wonderful accidents to have an airline pilot with a sort of a cowboy reputation whose name is Hoot Gibson, isn't it?

Someone commented that if his name was Harvey Korman, and he had three kids, and lived in New Jersey, this thing probably would have disappeared in about two days. That wasn't the case. His name was Hoot Gibson, and he was, in a sense, a mythical American western character.

In dealing with him, did you find him to correspond to that image as well, or was he a more complex character than that?

I think he was much more complex than that. He was one of the most fascinating, complex people I have ever met in my life, and people who might have criticized his life style said that in the end result he was one hell of a pilot. But he certainly did have those attributes of a Hoot Gibson.

Had you read *The Right Stuff*?

Yes, two things I did. I read parts of *The Right Stuff*, but I also read a book that I think helped me tremendously to gain knowledge of the pilot's psyche called *Fate Is the Hunter*, by Ernest Gann. He is really the foremost aviation writer in the country. He writes a lot of fiction involving planes, and he wrote *Fate Is the Hunter*, a book of non-fiction pieces about pilots and passengers and stewardesses involved in nightmarish-miracle situations involving airplane accidents.

Have you ever seen an airplane disaster movie?

No, I have never seen any of the big airplane disasters.

Have you seen the movie *Airplane*?

I think I have seen the movie *Airplane*. I think before this was written.

Did any of that play on your mind one way or another?

Not really. I thought the movie was pretty funny. But it didn't play on my mind. There is a passage in *The Right Stuff* in which Wolfe mi-

mics the pilot coming over the intercom. And that really was Gibson. The pilot with the western twang, kind of that laid back style that is sort of mixed with a lot of technological information. The way he described it was wonderful.

There's a section in *The Right Stuff* in which all these Navy Jets are going down all over the country, and it's always the pilot's fault, never the plane's fault. I mean that struck me. One of the miracles of the story: how three guys in a cockpit with a plane just completely careening out of control could actually do something.

Can I ask you a specific question about that? You have this conversation going on in the cockpit, and I was wondering whether there was any contradiction between all the pressures of these G forces and the seeming inability of some passengers even to move their arms, and the activity in the cockpit. That confused me a little bit.

Yes. I checked. I remember I called the aeromedical institute in Oklahoma City to check on the effects of these G forces, and they said indeed it would be true if the plane took as many G forces as it did that someone would be unable to move. In Gibson's case I know since he was an aerobatic pilot, he had experienced G forces similar to this and was able to do something.

It was a contradiction but then I sort of researched it a step further to see if it would be plausible. One woman had filed suit and I was able to see her medical record. She was in the hospital for a month. The doctor said she had experienced a definite physical problem so that was a way of verifying her story also.

OK. That perhaps leads us to another interesting problem of writing and reporting, and that is the question of attribution

which has become much discussed in the last year or so as a result of the Pulitzer controversies. There have been months of discussion about the need for attribution and when you use it, how you verify information. You've got a lot of information here coming from many different sources which you don't attribute.

Every fact in that story, if you pointed to it, I could attribute to investigative material or directly to the sources themselves. There was a very careful attempt made to do that.

Let me give you an example. This woman is experiencing these G forces and you describe her face being pulled back, her cheeks being pulled back, do you remember that? "The pressure was forcing her back into her seat, shoving her skin backwards, almost like someone had grabbed her cheeks and was trying to pull them back to see how much they would stretch." Where did that come from, for example?

There was a television show about this, and they had an actual clip of Air Force pilots experiencing G forces, and what happens. They had that effect and this was something that she described. In calling the aeromedical institute, they said indeed this would be true, that it would have this type of effect. They supplied me with various medical reports on Air Force pilots. You asked a question earlier about how could a pilot be functioning whereas a passenger could not? And they showed me a study of 100 Air Force pilots. There were some who blacked out a 2.8 G forces. There were others who were able to experience up to 9 G forces.

It's like how much booze you can tolerate or something like that?

Exactly, you know some are able to withstand a lot, some are not.

OK. Just above that, when the plane is starting to roll over. "In that fraction of a second, Hoot Gibson felt stark terror. The plane was rolling over and going in. He knew it. That was it. He was going to die. And take 88 other people down with him." Does that come from Hoot?

That comes from Hoot. He said that was the only moment in which he figured that was it, that we're going in. That's from Hoot himself.

You have already described how direct and simple and understated the narration is. You also use quotations with great selectivity and economy. Was that part of the understatement? Did you decide well I'm going to pick the very best quotations? "We're gonna die! We're gonna die!"

I don't know if you noticed it, but the story is a crosscut. It always goes from passenger to cockpit throughout the story, and the hardest thing to do on a written page is to create a sense of movement. You know I am trying to describe 44 seconds that visually you could understand in a second. On the written page it might not work out, so I think it had to be to the point. I am describing a very quick passage in time and I didn't want to dwell on anything for too long. I want to keep this thing moving with crosscuts, quick crosscuts back and forth, passenger to pilot, back to passenger, to pilot, to different parts of the airplane, whether it is someone in the last row or someone with a child in the middle of the coach.

You almost get a kind of slow-motion effect in the sense that you are recreating the event from many different perspectives al-